A Histo
Central

CW01431084

'In Brief': Books for Busy People

by Anne Davison

Copyright2020 Anne Davison

Cover Design by Karen Turner

CONTENTS

		Page
Preface		1
Chapter One:	Setting the Scene	3
Chapter Two:	The Achaemenid/Persian Empire	13
Chapter Three:	Alexander the Great	27
Chapter Four:	The Hellenistic World	49
Chapter Five:	Parthians, Kushans and Sassanids	64
Chapter Six:	The Arrival of Islam	81
Chapter Seven:	The Great Seljuk Empire	94
Chapter Eight:	The Mongols	111
Chapter Nine:	From Tamerlane to Nader Shah	128
Chapter Ten:	The Great Game	148
Chapter Eleven:	Soviet Central Asia	166
Epilogue		181
Who's Who		187
Works Referred to		193
About the Author		194

MAPS

	Page
Central Asia	5
Rivers and Mountains	7
Achaemenid Empire	13
Achaemenid Family Tree	21
Empire and Campaigns of Alexander the Great	31
Cities of Alexander the Great	33
Seleucid Family Tree	55
Parthian, Kushan and Sassanid Empires	64
Early Islamic Empires	82
Great Seljuk Empire	94
Genghis Khan Family Tree	120
Timurid Empire	132
Afghanistan	150
Significant Afghan Rulers	154

*****

PREFACE

The origin of this book stems from both my fascination with, and ignorance of, 'Central Asia'. The names, Samarkand, Bukhara and Khyber Pass have always conjured up images of remote desert cities, treacherous mountain passes, and above all, a spirit of danger and adventure. But I had little knowledge as to how these places fitted into the bigger picture of world history, or of their place in today's world. My attempts to answer these questions form the basis of this book.

Once having started the project, I was frequently asked, 'where, or what, is Central Asia?". It is a question that I continued to struggle with throughout working on the text. Finding a definition for 'Central Asia' is not helped by the fact that there is no consensus as to the geographical area forming 'Central Asia'. For example, UNESCO's definition includes Afghanistan, north-eastern Iran, northern and central Pakistan, northern India, western China, Mongolia and the former Soviet Central Asian republics. The most narrow, modern, definition for Central Asia, simply includes the five former Soviet Republics of Uzbekistan, Tajikistan, Turkmenistan, Kyrgyzstan and Khorasan.

The concept of Central Asia, as a distinct entity, is relatively modern. Consequently, research into the history of the region has inevitably been bound up with the histories of neighbouring powers, dynasties and invaders. As a result, much of the earlier part of the book focusses the great Persian/Iranian Empires that ruled the region, for example, the Achaemenids, the Sassanids and the Safavids. Other chapters cover the Turkic migrations, arrival of Islam and the invasion of the Mongols. The final chapters include the conflict between the imperial powers of Russia and Britain as each battled for influence in the region, known as the Great Game, as well as the 20th Century period of Soviet rule in Central Asia.

To attempt to cover so much material in a book of this size is admittedly ambitious. But this is the aim. In common with other titles in the 'In Brief' series, the book is written for the general reader who does not have the time, or inclination, to read a heavy academic tome. The intention is to provide an overview of Central Asia's complex history in an accessible and informative style, with maps and charts to help the reader navigate through the text.

While there will inevitably be gaps in a work of this size, it is hoped that the reader may be inspired to further reading on the subject. Therefore, for those interested, a short selection of the main works that have been consulted is provided at the back of the book, as well as a list of the main characters referred to.

Finally, I would like to thank those friends and colleagues who have given of their time to read through various chapters, to proof read the script, as well as to offer helpful comments.

*****

CHAPTER ONE
Setting the Scene

From ancient times, Central Asia has formed a land bridge between Europe and East Asia. Along its great highways, known as the Silk Roads, silk, paper and spices travelled westwards from China and India, while furs, wools, gold and silver from Europe went eastwards. Apart from trade, ideas, philosophies and religions were carried by traders and travellers in both directions. And along the thousands of miles of route, what began as simple trading posts, became wealthy cities such as Samarkand, Bukhara and Tashkent in today's Uzbekistan.

For most of its history, the region we now refer to as Central Asia, formed part of major Empire such as the Achaemenids or the Safavids. At other times, territory was held in vassalage to more powerful neighbours, for example, the Chinese, the Russians and more recently the British. Large parts of the interior, that were more inaccessible, were ruled by independent tribal leaders, emirs, khans and kings.

The term 'Central Asia' was first coined in the 19th Century by the renowned German explorer Alexander von Humboldt, who had travelled from Russia to the Altai Mountains near the Chinese border in 1829 as a guest of the Tsar. At about the same time, British and Russian agents were exploring the region in the context of the Great Game, which was a 19th Century contest between the two powers for control over the region. (See Chapter 10) Before then, very little was known in the West of the topography and geography of the vast region that stretches from Russia in the North to Afghanistan in the South, and Iran in the West to China in the East. Any knowledge that people did have, might have been limited to tales of the Silk Road, the terrors of Tamerlane or the fabled Christian King of Central Asia known as Prester John.

The Chinese, however, were sending missions of exploration into Central Asia long before the West. As early as the 2nd Century BCE, the Han Emperor Wu sent his official Zhang Qian on a fact-finding tour into the region, primarily with thoughts of future colonisation. Zhang travelled as far as the valleys of Fergana and Bactria which straddle modern Afghanistan, Tajikistan, Uzbekistan and parts of Northern Pakistan.

Zhang returned to China with reports of sophisticated cities and advanced cultures. He speaks of a powerful 'blood-sweating' horse and a two-humped camel. The Fergana horse, also known as the 'heavenly horse', eventually became a prized import from Central Asia into China. It is thought that the 'blood-sweating' was the result of an infection caused by a tiny worm that buried beneath the animal's skin.

Zhang's travels opened up Central Asian markets to Chinese trade and he is credited for playing a key role in the development of the Silk Road through Central Asia to Europe. Today, at a time when China is reinventing the Silk Road with its ambitious Belt and Road initiative, a project aimed at linking 152 countries across Europe, Asia, Latin America and Africa, Zhang Qian is held up as a national hero, an icon of early Chinese exploration.

Today, the term Central Asia, as narrowly defined, covers the former Soviet Republics of Kazakhstan, Kyrgyzstan, Tajikistan, Turkmenistan and Uzbekistan, collectively known as 'the stans'; 'stan' being the Persian word for 'land of'. Ethnicity has also been used to define Central Asia. Using this methodology, Afghanistan, parts of Pakistan and Siberia and the Xinjiang Uyghur Autonomous Region of China are also considered to be part of Central Asia, because their peoples are of Eastern Turkic, Eastern Iranian or Mongolian ethnicities.

The land

The region contains some of the most inhospitable parts of the world, including high mountains, vast deserts and barren steppe.

The most significant characteristic of Central Asia, that has shaped the region's history, is that it is completely landlocked. The city of Urumqi, in China's Xinjiang Province, marks the world's furthermost point from any ocean, otherwise known as the Eurasian pole of inaccessibility. The region also falls within an earthquake zone that runs from China to Turkey, across the

5

Mediterranean and the Atlantic, to the Caribbean. Consequently, earthquakes are common along the ridges of the Hindu Kush and the mountains of Iran. The grass steppe of Central Asia, along with the steppe lands of Eastern Europe, together form the geographic zone known as the Eurasian Steppe.

Central Asia also contains remote deserts. The Kyzylkum (meaning Red Sand), measuring some 115,000 square miles, is located between the rivers Amu Darya (Oxus) and Syr Darya (Jaxartes) and falls within Kazakhstan, Uzbekistan and Turkmenistan. The Karakum (meaning Black Sand), measuring some 135,000 square miles, occupies around 70% of the land of Turkmenistan.

Taking the broader definition for the region, the Taklamakan Desert and Dzungaria in the Xinjiang Province of China, fall within Central Asia. The Taklamakan, which covers an area of some 130,000 square miles, was annexed by the Qing Dynasty of China in 1789. It is linked in the East to the Gobi Desert and includes the Tarim Basin, 85% of which consists of shifting sands. The Tarim also sits within a rain shadow of the Himalayas, resulting in a dryness that makes it extremely cold. Due to the inhospitality of the Tarim Basin, the early Silk Roads between China and Central Asia skirted the desert, taking either a Southern or Northern route. Today, the People's Republic of China has built two highways across the desert and there are plans to construct a railroad. The desert is also a popular location for film and TV productions.

Dzungaria forms the northern part of the Xinjian Province and extends into western Mongolia and eastern Kazakhstan. Although united with the Tarim Basin into the autonomous province of Xinjian, it is a separate entity in terms of history and culture. Whereas Tarim is inhabited predominently by Turkic Muslim Uyghurs, the people of Dzungaria are mainly Tibetan Buddhist Mongol. While the Tarim Basin is 85% desert sand, Dzungaria enjoys a relatively moist climate and is semi-desert. The city of Urumqi, renowned for being the most remote city from any sea, is located in Dzungaria, as is the Turfan Depression, China's hottest and driest region, which at minus

500 feet below sea level, is one of the lowest depressions in the world

The Chinese have invested in industry, infrastructure and modern communications in Dzungaria, as well as a road and rail route, known as the Dzungarian Gate, which connects with Kazakhstan. In previous centuries, traders generally took the southern Silk Road along the south side of the Tarim Basin towards Fergana. Migrants, on the other hand, took the northern Silk Road through Dzungaria, as did the Mongols when they burst out of Mongolia in the 13th Century.

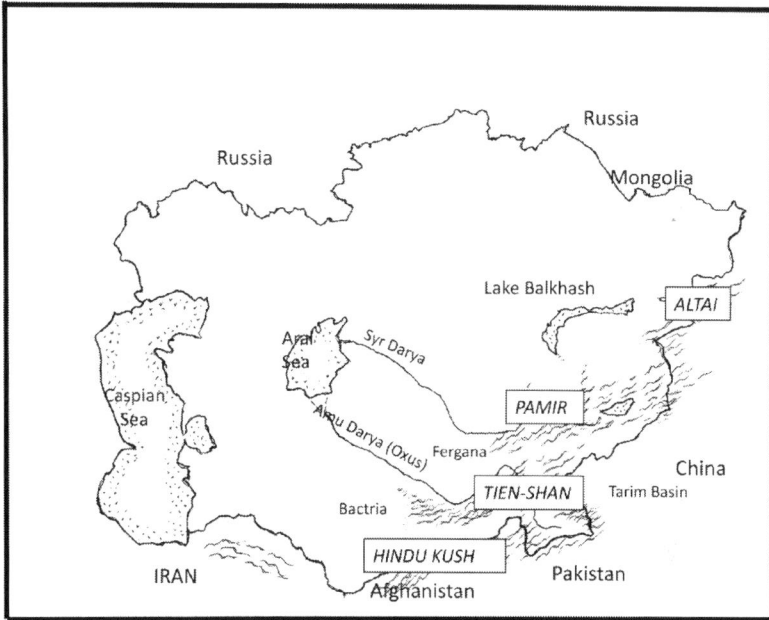

The mountain ranges, namely the Altai, the Pamirs, the Tien-Shan and the Hindu Kush, form a natural barrier between Central Asia and China in the East and Pakistan and Afghanistan in the South. For centuries, the only land access to China and India was through high mountain passes. Travellers to India took the treacherous Khyber Pass passing through today's Afghanistan and Pakistan.

The mountain ranges are separated by high plateaus and the foothills on the western side fall away into valleys, sometimes referred to as bays. One of the most famous of these bays is Fergana Valley in modern Uzbekistan, which was the birthplace of Babur, the first Mughal Emperor of India. The ancient region of Bactria, which was settled by followers of Alexander the Great (see Chapter 3) is located in another bay, or valley. These fertile valleys are watered from two main rivers, the Amu Darya and Syr Darya, which rise in the Pamir mountains and run northwest into the Aral Sea. During the Soviet period, industrial and agricultural projects were established in the delta region of the Aral Sea and irrigation for these projects has caused a dramatic drop in the water level in both the Aral Sea and Lake Balkhash.

From ancient times, the fertile valleys of Fergana and Bactria have attracted settled communities and provided hospitality for travellers. The area formed part of the early Silk Road and the location of the ancient cities of Tashkent, Samarkand, Khiva and Bukhara, are all within today's Uzbekistan.

The Iranian-Speaking peoples

Although we have no written records of the people who first inhabited Central Asia, we have archaeological evidence of the various tribes. These tribes can be broadly divided into two main linguistic-ethnic groups; the Iranian speaking group, and the Turkic speaking group. Apart from Iran, Iranian speaking peoples can be found today in the Central Asian countries of Afghanistan, Pakistan, Tajikistan, Uzbekistan, Turkmenistan and the Xinjiang Province of China.

The origins of the Iranian speaking peoples can be traced back to the Caucasian Indo-Iranians of the Sintashta culture that existed on the borders of Central Asia and Eastern Europe between 2100-1800 BCE. It is here that archaeologists discovered evidence of the first spoked wheel and tombs used for sacrificial horse burial. The Sintashta was superseded by the Andronovo, a culture that absorbed many Sintashta characteristics and innovations, including the war chariot. The Andronovo then spread from the Eurasian Steppe to Western Siberia around 2000-900 BCE.

Between 1800-1600 BCE a group known as the Indo-Iranians split from the Iranians and migrated into Anatolia in the West and the northern part of South Asia, including Afghanistan, Pakistan, India and Nepal. The remaining Iranians moved into the region of today's Iran. It is thought that these large-scale migrations were caused by climate change, leading to water shortage.

The migration of the Indo-Aryans into northern India has been associated with the collapse of the Indus Valley Harappan civilisation. The British archaeologist, Sir Mortimer Wheeler, suggested in the 1950s that the sophisticated urban civilisation of Harappa and Mohenjo Daro was destroyed by an invading Indo-Aryan tribe from Central Asia.

Wheeler's theory that the Indo-Aryans caused the destruction of the Indus Valley civilisation was based largely on the discovery of skulls that he believed showed evidence of warfare. However, his claim has been challenged more recently by other scholars on the grounds that the skulls were of a later period and that erosion, rather than violence, caused the damage to the skulls.

With the arrival of the Aryans into Northern India, the darker skinned Dravidians of the Indus Valley migrated southwards. It was at this time that the word 'Aryan' became linked to the meaning of 'noble'. Furthermore, as the lighter-skinned Aryans came to dominate the more passive Dravidians, the concept of a caste system based on colour began to take form.

It is possible that the horse culture and chariot warfare of the Eurasian Steppe migrated into the Indus Valley region along with the Aryans. The *Ashvamedha,* for example, which forms part of the ancient Hindu Vedas, is a sacred text laying down the ritual to be followed for performing the horse sacrifice. Also, the *Mahabharata,* which forms part of the Vedas, is an epic tale on the ethics of warfare. War chariots are a major feature of the epic and two of the main characters are Arjuna the warrior archer with Lord Krishna as his mentor and charioteer.

The Turkic-speaking peoples

Turkic-speaking peoples inhabit an area from Anatolia and the Caucasus in the West, across Siberia and Central Asia, to China in the East. Apart from Turkey, large communities of Turkic speaking people live in today's Azerbaijan, Uzbekistan, Kazakhstan, Turkmenistan and Kyrgyzstan.

It is thought that the earliest Turkic speaking tribes may have been members of the Xiongnu nomadic tribal confederation that ruled the region of today's Mongolia between the 3rd Century BCE and 1st Century CE, a period that was contemporary with the Qin and Han Dynasties of China. According to Chinese historians, such as *Sima Qin,* the Chinese had a volatile relationship with the Xiongnu and the decision of the Han to strengthen the Great Wall was partly aimed at keeping the aggressive Xiongnu tribes at bay.

Later Tang historians described the Turkic Kyrgyz tribes as being fair-skinned, with red hair and green or blue eyes, suggesting their Caucasian origins. They could equally have been descendants of Alexander the Great's armies, since Alexander had penetrated as far East as Sogdiana by 326 BCE. Sogdiana was an Iranian civilisation that existed in Central Asia between the 6th Century BCE and 11th Century CE. Furthermore, Chinese records refer to the Kyrgyz tribes doing trade along the Silk Road with the Sogdians,

By the 6th Century CE, the Gokturks, meaning 'Celestial Turks' or 'Blue Turks' had come to prominence and established a Turkic Khaganate north of the Altai Mountains. The colour Turquoise became symbolic of the Turkic tribes of Central Asia and the word turquoise is derived from the French word for Turkish.

The earliest examples of the ancient Turkic language in the written form, appeared as inscriptions on steles. The first to be discovered were the 'Bain Tsokto' steles that date from around 700 CE and are located near Ulaanbaatar, the capital city of today's Mongolia. The inscriptions on the steles record revolts and wars between Tang China and the Oghuz Turks.

The other inscriptions of significance are known as the 'Orkhon Inscriptions', also located in central Mongolia. They were erected in the early 8th Century CE in honour of two Turkic princes. Written in both Chinese and Old Turkic, they tell the history of the Turks including their subjugation under the Chinese and liberation by Ilterish Khaghan, founder of the Second Turkic Khaganate. The inscriptions are now part of the Orkon Valley UNESCO world heritage site and archaeologists from across the Turkic speaking world are still excavating the area.

Over the following centuries, waves of Turkic people migrated westwards. Three of these groups had a major impact on the history of Central Asia. First, the Seljuks, who were a branch of the Oghuz Yabgu State that ruled Kazakhstan between 750-1055 CE. The Seljuks established an empire that, at its greatest extent, covered an area from Anatolia to the border with China and the Indus Valley (see Chapter 7). It was the invasion of the Seljuks into Byzantine territory in the 11th Century, that led to the First Crusade.

The next migration, in the 14th Century, was the Turco-Mongol Timurids. Under their leader Timur, better known in the West as Tamerlane, the Timurids established a vast empire covering Central Asia, Pakistan, parts of India and the Levant (see Chapter 9).

The third major group were descendants of the Kayi tribe of the Oghuz Turks. Taking their name from their leader, Osman Gazi, they became known as the Ottomans. The Ottoman Empire lasted from 1299 to 1922, when it was dissolved following World War One.

Conclusion

Apart from the ex-Soviet Republics of Turkmenistan, Uzbekistan, Tajikistan, Kazakhstan and Kyrgyzstan, it is somewhat arbitrary as to which other countries constitute Central Asia. There is a temptation to include all countries with the suffix 'stan', meaning 'land of'. In this case we would include Pakistan, Afghanistan, Kurdistan etc. Another method for deciding on the boundaries of Central Asia is to take ethnicity as the defining factor, for example Eastern Turkic, Eastern Iranian or Mongolian. Using this methodology, we would include the Xinjiang Province in Western China, and parts of Western Mongolia.

When trying to unravel the history of Central Asia, it is difficult to limit the region to the ex-Soviet Republics, which in any case are modern constructs. Events in history do not necessarily respect boundaries. People migrate, armies invade, nations are conquered or become vassal states and boundaries constantly change.

This is particularly true of Central Asia. The region has experienced invasion and occupation from all directions; the Persians and Greeks from the West and the Russians from the North. From the East, despite the formidable mountain range, came the Mongolians and Chinese, and in the 19th Century, the British invaded Central Asia from British India.

For centuries, the landlocked region also provided a bridge for trade between East and West. Known as the Silk Road, it was in fact, many roads, or portions of road, that linked towns and cities from Mongolia, China and India, to the Mediterranean and Europe.

Finally, there were migrations, the first being the Indo-Iranians who migrated from the Caucasus to the Indus Valley in today's Pakistan. Later, waves of Turkic-speaking nomadic tribes migrated from Mongolia westwards, the last one being the tribe of Osman I, who founded the Ottoman Dynasty.

While the majority of the people of Central Asia are Iranian, or Turkic-Speaking, they are ethnically diverse. The region today is multi-cultural, multi-ethnic, multi-religious and multi-linguistic, reflecting its rich and often turbulent history.

*****

CHAPTER TWO

The Achaemenid/ First Persian Empire

The Achaemenid Empire, also known as the First Persian Empire, was founded by Cyrus the Great in 550 BCE and it lasted until 330 BCE, when the Persian King of Kings, Darius III, was defeated by Alexander the Great. At its greatest extent, the Empire covered an area from the Balkans in the West, to the Indus Valley in the East. It was the largest Empire the world had yet known.

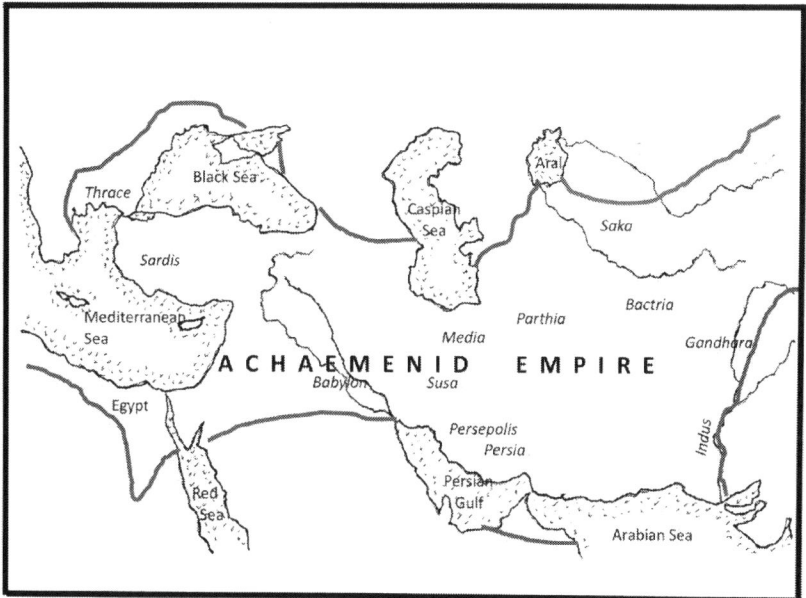

It is sometimes said that the history of Central Asia really begins with the founding of the Achaemenid Empire, because from this time onwards we have written records of events. We get most of our information from the Greeks, who were the scholars of the day. At that time, unlike other nations, the Greeks possessed a written language and produced a wealth of literature. The written language of the Persians, on the other hand, was limited to the religious texts of early Zoroastrianism. Apart from only being accessible to the priests, the script did not suit a written narrative.

The two Greek historians best known for providing us with a narrative of the events surrounding Cyrus the Great, are Herodotus (c 484-c 425 BCE) and Xenophon (c 431-c 354 BCE). Both were men of wealth and status. Herodotus was a philosopher and scholar and he is often referred to as the 'Father of History'. Xenophon, on the other hand, was a military man and great general. Coming from different backgrounds, each focussed on a different aspect of the narrative surrounding Cyrus. While they differ in detail and were undoubtedly both prone to exaggeration, it is their portrayal of Cyrus, and description of the Achaemenid Empire, that has come down to us through the centuries.

Herodotus, who was born in Halicarnassus, modern day Bodrum in Turkey, learned to read and write at an early age. As was usual for a boy from his background, he also studied philosophy and the works of the great poets, historians and orators. It was a time when public entertainment included not just games, races and wrestling, but also plays and poetry reading. Famous orators also engaged in public debate, while others enthralled audiences with tales of travels to far-off lands.

While Herodotus had a thirst for all kinds of knowledge, he was particularly inspired by stories of distant places. He decided to embark on his own journeys of discovery so that he could entertain the Athenians with tales of his exploits on his return. He travelled to Egypt, Libya, the Levant and then eastwards into Assyria, Babylonia and Scythia, which was a vast territory north of the Caspian and Aral Seas. While in Assyria and Babylonia he gathered material for his stories from the local population, as well as from travelling merchants and mercenary soldiers.

Xenophon was born in Athens about fifty years after the birth of Herodotus. He had a similar education to Herodotus, but at the age of 22 he joined a 13,000 strong Greek expeditionary force of the Persian Governor of Asia Minor, known as Cyrus the Younger (not to be confused with Cyrus the Great). At the time, Cyrus the Younger was building up an army in order to overthrow his brother, Artaxerxes, who was then King of the small kingdom of Persia.

The allied force of Cyrus the Younger was defeated by Artaxerxes. Cyrus was killed and most of his men either died in battle or fled. However, 10,000 men of the Greek contingent survived. After refusing to surrender to Artaxerxes, and finding themselves trapped in dangerous territory, the army decided to retreat. Under the command of Xenophon, the Greek troops commenced a 215-day march through unfamiliar and hostile territory from Mesopotamia to the Black Sea. Known as the Retreat of the Ten Thousand, it was a feat that made Xenophon famous as a military strategist.

Whilst in Asia, both Herodotus and Xenophon gained valuable information about Cyrus the Great and also the Persian Empire; Herodotus through his fact-finding journeys, and Xenophon while on military campaign. Historians have questioned their reliability in terms of factual truth, but all historians can be accused of a degree of bias. It could be that since Herodotus was partly writing for the entertainment of the Athenians, he was likely to embellish his accounts and is therefore less reliable than Xenophon. What cannot be denied, however, is that their writings have survived two thousand years and remain a primary source of information on the Achaemenid Empire.

Cyrus the Great: ruled 559-530 BCE

Cyrus II, known as 'the Great', was born around 598 BCE in Anshan, Persia. His father, Cambyses I was King of Anshan and his mother, Mandane, was the daughter of Astyages, King of the Median Empire. At the time, Persia, also referred to as Persis, was a small vassal state of the Medes. It was located in the modern region of Fars, Iran, from which comes the name Farsi or the Farsi language.

According to Herodotus, Cyrus spent several years with his grandfather, Astyages, at the Median court when he was a boy.

The experience gave the young boy an insight into the workings of the Median Empire, which was later to prove invaluable. He is described as *'being a very beautiful boy, tall and graceful in form and his countenance was striking and expressive. He was very frank and open in his disposition and character, speaking honestly, and without fear...He was extremely kind hearted and amiable'.* (Jacob Abbott, *Cyrus the Great Makers of History*)

When Cyrus was about twelve, he left the Median court to return to Persia, where he entered the demanding Persian education system. In every Persian city, males of all ages would gather at different times each day in the central square. They were divided into four groups: boys (under 16); youths (16-26); men (27-50) and elders (over 50). Each group had its own prescribed set of duties.

The boys ate together, rather than at home and their main task was to study the principles of justice, law, rules and regulations. They were also taught to wrestle, run and hunt. The youths were responsible for guarding all public buildings as well as undergoing a demanding military training. They also accompanied the King on his hunting expeditions. The adult men provided military service and were the backbone of the army, while the elders acted as public servants, performing civic duties as well as acting as official advisers to the younger men.

Expansion of the Empire

In 559 BCE, Cyrus succeeded his father as King. Under his rule Persia gained power, while the Median Empire, ruled by the ageing and corrupt Astyages, went into decline. In 549 BCE, Cyrus manipulated the peaceful overthrow of Astyages and became King of the Medes as well as the Persians. Through further diplomacy, he was able to win over the Median vassal states of the Bactrians, Parthians and Saka and he installed his relatives as *satraps,* or governors, over each region. The provinces ruled by the *satraps*, were autonomous but they were all expected to pay tribute to Cyrus, known as the King of Kings, as well as provide troops when necessary. It was a system that would last throughout a number of Imperial dynasties until the arrival of Islam in the 7th Century and the fall of the Sasanian Empire in 651 CE.

Having peacefully annexed the Median Empire, together with its vassal states, Cyrus turned his attention to Lydia, which roughly corresponds to the Western part of today's Turkey. Croesus, King of Lydia, had previously attacked the Persian city of Pteria in Cappadocia and Cyrus was determined to take it back. The Lydians were forced to retreat from Pteria to their capital city of Sardis and in 547 BCE, Croesus was finally defeated at the Battle of Thumbra. It is said that Cyrus won the battle because he deployed his camels against the Lydian horses. Apparently, the horses, which were put off by the strong smell of the camels, simply turned and fled. Lydia then became one more *satrapy* of the Achaemenid Empire. Between 546 and 540 BCE, Lycia, Cilicia, Phoenicia, Syria, Judea and Arabia Petraea, were all incorporated into the Persian Empire as provinces or *satrapies.*

Cyrus then turned eastwards and conquered the city of Susa near the River Tigris in today's Iraq, before marching on to the great city of Babylon on the River Euphrates. Herodotus gives a detailed description of the city as it must have been seen by Cyrus. He tells how the whole country, which was very fertile, was watered by the river and numerous canals. He describes King Belshazzar's palace, the parks and 'hanging gardens' and he tells of the magnificent buildings that were embellished with images of giant-sized exotic animals.

Cyrus managed to take the city of Babylon without resorting to violence. He ordered his men to dig trenches so that he could divert the water away from the river into nearby canals. When the water level in the river dropped sufficiently for his troops to wade through the shallow river, he was able to gain access to the city unchallenged.

The Cyrus Cylinder

In 1879, the Assyro-British archaeologist Hormuzd Rassam, discovered a baked-clay cylinder in the foundations of the ancient Marduk temple of Babylon. It is now known as the Cyrus Cylinder and is kept in the British Museum.

The cylinder, which is only 23 cm long and 11 cm wide, describes how, on October 29th, 539 BCE, Cyrus peacefully entered the city of Babylon and assumed the title *'king of Babylon, king of Sumer and Akkad, king of the four corners of the world'*. The inscription on the cylinder, which is written in Akkadian, also proclaims his decrees, namely that throughout his Empire there should be racial, linguistic and religious equality; that all deported people would be allowed to return home and that all destroyed temples should be restored. It has been described as the world's first Charter of Human Rights.

According to the Hebrew Scriptures, it was during this time that many Israelites were being held in captivity in Babylon, having been captured by the Babylonian King Nebuchadnezzar. The event is known as the 'Babylonian Exile', or 'Babylonian Captivity'. Under the decree of Cyrus, the Israelites would have been eligible for repatriation. The Hebrew Bible (Ezra 1:1-8), appears to confirm that this did indeed happen:

'In the first year of Cyrus king of Persia, in order to fulfil the word of the Lord spoken by Jeremiah, the Lord moved the heart of Cyrus king of Persia to make a proclamation throughout his realm and also to put it in writing:

    "This is what Cyrus king of Persia says:

    "'The Lord, the God of heaven, has given me all the kingdoms of the earth and he has appointed me to build a temple for him at Jerusalem in Judah. Any of his people among you may go up to Jerusalem in Judah and build the temple of the Lord, the God of Israel, the God who is in Jerusalem, and may their God be with them. And in any locality where survivors may now be living, the people are to provide them with silver and gold, with goods and livestock, and with freewill offerings for the temple of God in Jerusalem.'"

The Hebrew Scriptures also describe how Cyrus returned to the Jews all the temple artefacts, including hundreds of gold and silver dishes, that had been stolen by King Nebuchadnezzar. Rembrandt's famous painting *'Belshazzar's Feast'* is set within this context. It shows how Nebuchadnezzar's son, Belshazzar, was feasting off the stolen dishes when the hand of God appeared on the wall, warning him that his kingdom was about to fall. The prophesy was fulfilled when the Babylonians fell to the Persians. The story of Belshazzar's Feast has long inspired both artists and musicians; for example, the 19th Century British painter, John Martin and the 20th Century composer William Walton.

Cyrus's final campaign was in 530 BCE against the Massagetae, a tribe related to the Scythians who lived in the southern steppe region of today's Kazakhstan and Uzbekistan. Initially Cyrus sent an offer of marriage to the ruler, Empress Tomyris, hoping in this way to bring the Massagetae into his Empire. When she rejected his offer, the two sides prepared for war. They were separated by the river Syr Darya (Jaxartes). Despite the Persians' formidable tower boats, the Massagetae, led by their Empress, defeated the Persians and Cyrus was killed in battle.

He was buried in his capital city of Pasargadae, located in today's Fars Province of Iran. Although the original city is now in ruins, Cyrus's tomb has remained largely intact and since 2015 it has been a UNESCO World Heritage Site. According to Plutarch, the tomb bore the inscription:

> *"O man, whoever you are and wherever you come from, for I know you will come, I am Cyrus who won the Persians their Empire. Do not therefore begrudge me this bit of earth that covers my bones."*

The Achaemenid Army

We get a certain amount of information about the Achaemenid army from both Herodotus and Xenophon. Another reliable source comes from historical artefacts. The ancient capital city of Persepolis, for example, provides a wealth of information. Surviving inscriptions on ancient monuments testify to the multi-ethnic nature of the Empire. Elaborate carvings show soldiers from Media, Parthia, Persia and Bactria, each wearing their own distinctive uniforms, headgear and arms.

As the Achaemenids expanded into a world empire, troop levies were imposed on newly conquered people, resulting in a multi-ethnic imperial standing army. While the Persians always remained in the majority, the Medes, who were the second largest group, provided the Generals and Imperial Guard. Smaller contingencies came from the more recently conquered regions. Those closest to Persepolis, the imperial capital, provided the largest number of troops, but paid less in tribute. Correspondingly, those nations on the periphery of the Empire, provided a smaller number of troops but paid a higher tribute.

It was normal for Greek mercenaries to be in the service of the Persians. As mentioned earlier, Xenophon had joined a Greek expeditionary force to fight on behalf of the Persian Governor of Asia Minor. However, under Cyrus the Great, Greek mercenary units became an official part of the Persian army and were given free board as well as wages. The presence of Greek soldiers stationed in Persia, was one factor that later enabled the spread of Greek culture eastwards across Central Asia after the conquest of Alexander the Great. (See Chapter Three)

The Achaemenid army was made up of Infantry, Cavalry, Camels and occasionally elephants. Chariots were used by the nobility as well as their wives and concubines. Baggage wagons and camp followers brought up the rear. The Imperial banner, in the form of a golden eagle, was carried in front and every campaign was accompanied by *Magi* (priests) who were responsible for carrying the holy fire, the religious symbol of the Zoroastrian god *Ahura Mazda*.

The soldiers wore distinctive uniforms, reflecting their place of origin. They also wore metal helmets and padded jackets with metal plating on the outside. While the foot soldiers carried short swords, spears and a bow and quiver, the cavalry carried longer swords and javelins. However, because there was no saddle or stirrup at that time, the heavily armoured cavalrymen were easily thrown from their horse.

Darius the Great: ruled 522-486 BCE

Cyrus the Great was succeeded by his son Cambyses II, who ruled until 522 BCE, at which time Darius I, known as the Great, came to the throne.

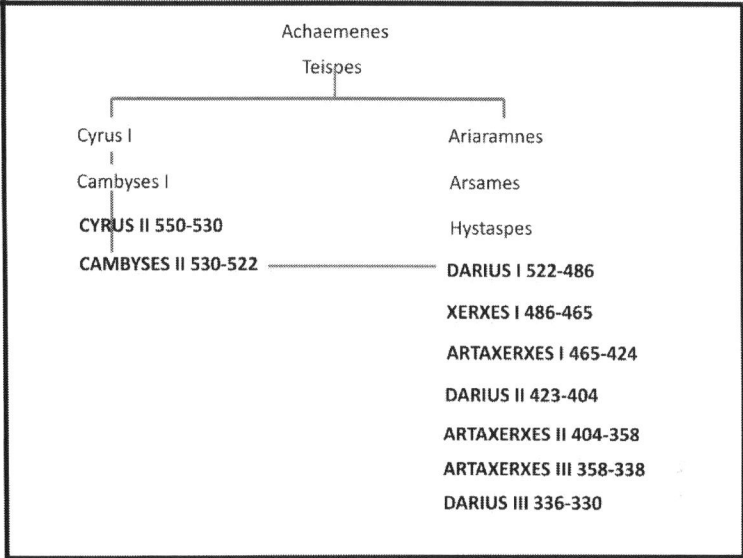

```
                           Achaemenes
                            Teispes
           ┌──────────────────────┴──────────────────────┐
       Cyrus I                                       Ariaramnes

       Cambyses I                                    Arsames

       CYRUS II 550-530                              Hystaspes

       CAMBYSES II 530-522 ················· DARIUS I 522-486

                                             XERXES I 486-465

                                             ARTAXERXES I 465-424

                                             DARIUS II 423-404

                                             ARTAXERXES II 404-358

                                             ARTAXERXES III 358-338

                                             DARIUS III 336-330
```

While Cyrus founded the imperial army, it was under Darius I that the Achaemenid navy grew to be the greatest sea power in the known world. As the Empire expanded into the Levant and as far West as Egypt, the region's most experienced sailors and ship-builders came under Persian rule. The ship-yards at Sidon, in today's Lebanon, built ships for the Persians that could carry as many as 300 men. The sailors came from Egypt, Greece and Phoenicia. Persian ships sailed down the Persian Gulf and plied rivers as far East as the River Indus. As well as carrying troops, the ships also carried goods for trade.

During the first year of Darius's rule he faced rebellions from various parts of the Empire. Once these were put down, however, he began to consolidate and further expand his Empire. He improved the *satrap* system that had been put in place by Cyrus, by dividing his empire into 24 provinces, each with various degrees of autonomy. He built roads with post-houses and caravanserai stationed at regular intervals along the route where travellers, and especially couriers, could obtain both lodging and fresh horses. He also introduced a uniform system of weights and measures as well as the use of Aramaic as the official imperial language.

Until the reign of Darius, the only coinage in use in the region was that of the Lydians, who were possibly the first people in the West to mint coins. By adding an image of the Persian king to the Lydian coin, Darius introduced the official Imperial coinage. The Daric, that is still in use today, may have been named after Darius.

Darius continued his expansionist campaigns by first conquering Egypt and parts of today's Balkans. Then in 516 BCE, he subdued large swathes of Central Asia, including Afghanistan, as well as Gandhara and Taxila in today's Pakistan. With his conquest of the Eastern tribes, he not only acquired hardened warriors for his army, but he also gained valuable mineral mines. While in the East, he commissioned Greek explorers to sail down the Indus into the Indian Ocean and round to the Persian Gulf. His intention was to gain as much information as possible of the coastline, with the ultimate aim of further conquest.

Greece and the Ionian islands presented the greatest prize for Darius, but he was not yet ready to attempt an invasion. Instead, in 513 BCE, he turned his attention to the Scythians, tribal people living North of the Danube and Black Sea. The Scythians posed a threat to the Persians. They were extremely warlike and have been linked with the mythical tribe of Amazon women warriors.

In order to defend his Empire against the Scythians, Darius knew that he needed to control the Bosphorus, the narrow strip of water that separates Europe from Asia that is located in modern Istanbul. Having secured the Bosphorus he could then control Thrace and advance towards the Danube. Furthermore, from Thrace, he would then be in a stronger position to launch a later invasion into Greece.

In advance of the main campaign into Europe, he sent two contingents of troops and engineers on ahead. The first contingent built a bridge of boats across the Bosphorus. The second contingent sailed through the Black Sea to the mouth of the River Danube. After sailing upstream, the Persians built another bridge of boats across the Danube. According to Herodotus, Darius was now able to cross from Asia Minor into Europe with a force of 600 Greek ships and an army of some 700,000 to 800,000 men.

After facing no serious opposition from the Scythians, Darius returned to Asia Minor with his army virtually intact. He did, however, leave some 80,000 troops behind in Thrace and Macedonia in order to remind them of their vassalage status. The subjection of Macedonia to Persian rule was later to have serious repercussions for the Achaemenid Empire.

Ionian Revolt

The Ionians, who were Greek tribal people living along the west coast of modern Turkey, were placed under the Persian *satrap* of Sardis. The *satrap* then appointed *tyrants*, who were local Greeks, to rule over the people. The *tyrants* were cruel, despotic masters and in 499 BCE, the people rose up against them in what became known as the Ionian Revolt. It was to be the first phase of the Greco-Persian Wars, that lasted until 449 BCE.

The Ionians were supported by many of the Greek City states, that provided hundreds of Greek ships and 120,000 men to support the rebellion against Persian Rule. With the help of the Athenians, the Ionians attacked and burned Sardis. In response, Darius's army chased the Ionians back towards the coast where they were soundly beaten at the Battle of Ephesus. But this did not stop the rebellion, which continued to spread along the coast and islands of the Aegean Sea as far as Cyprus.

In 494 BCE, with the help of naval fleets from Egypt, Cilicia and Phoenicia, Darius was able to finally put down the revolt. But he was determined to punish the Athenians for supporting the revolt. He first strengthened his grip on Thrace and Macedonia and he gained the submission of several Greek City States. When Athens and Sparta refused to submit, he launched his first invasion of the Greek mainland.

In August 490 BCE, 600 Persian triremes, carrying around 25,000 troops landed on a beach near Marathon in Greece. Having only around 10,000 men, the Athenians sent a messenger to Sparta appealing for help. Despite the failure to get help from the Spartans, who were in the middle of religious festivities at the time, the Athenians succeeded in defeating the Persians.

According to Herodotus, Persian casualties included around 6,400 dead with seven ships destroyed, while the Athenians only lost 192 men. Modern historians put the Persian casualties at between 4,000 to 5,000 dead with the Athenian loss between 1,000 to 3,000.

Herodotus identified the messenger who ran to Sparta seeking help as Pheidippides. Others claim that Pheidippides ran the 25 miles from the battle field to Athens to announce the victory over the Persians. Whatever the truth may be, the legacy of the Battle of Marathon remains with us today in the form of the Marathon run which was incorporated into the first modern Olympic Games in 1896. Today Marathon runs take place in many countries around the world but rather than 25 miles, the fixed distance is now 26 miles, 385 yards.

Death of Darius

Following the humiliating defeat at Marathon, the Persians returned to Asia Minor. Darius immediately started to plan another invasion of Greece, but he was interrupted by rebellions in Egypt. In October 486 BCE, he died of natural causes at the age of 64.

The life of Darius is immortalised in the *Behistun* Inscription that is carved into a rockface at Mount Behistun in the Kermanshah Province of Iran. The inscription, that is thought to have been commissioned by Darius, is approximately 15 metres high and 25 metres wide and is carved into a limestone cliff that is located on the ancient road that connected the capital cities of Babylonia and Media.

A life-size relief of Darius shows the King of Kings holding a bow as a sign of kingship. The illustration also shows a line of men with ropes rounds their necks, each with different clothing and hairstyles. These are thought to represent the conquered people who were incorporated into the Achaemenid Empire.

The cuneiform script is written in three languages: Old Persian, Elamite and Babylonian. It includes the lineage of Darius the Great and a list of his campaigns. According to the text, Darius says:

> *These are the countries which are subject unto me, and by the grace of Ahuramazda I am king of them: Persia, Elam, Babylonia, Assyria, Arabia, Egypt, the countries by the sea, Lydia, the Greeks, Media, Armenia, Cappadocia, Parthia, Drangiana, Aria, Chorasmia, Bactria, Sogdia, Gandhara, Scythia, Sattagydia, Arachosia, Maka; twenty-three lands in all.*

Some 150 years later, all this would be lost by Darius's namesake, Darius III, when he fled the battlefield in the face of Alexander the Great.

Conclusion

At its greatest extent, the Achaemenid Empire, also known as the First Persian Empire, covered an area from Egypt and the Balkans in the West to the Indus Valley in the East. It was the largest empire the world had yet known.

Evidence of Persian rule in Central Asia and as far east as Afghanistan, can be found from archaeological sites and historical artefacts, with perhaps the *Behistun* Inscription providing the clearest indication of the extent of the Empire. The writings of the Greek historians Herodotus and Xenophon provide us with a lineage of the kings, details of the Achaemenid army and an account of the military campaigns and conquests.

When Cyrus, as King of Persia, peacefully overthrew his grandfather Astyages, King of the Medes, in 550 BCE, he automatically inherited the Median vassal states. In this way he became ruler of vast territories, styled himself King of Kings, and is credited as founder of the Achaemenid Empire.

Cyrus earned the synonym 'the Great' because of his just policies towards those he conquered and his enlightened approach to those he ruled. This is epitomised in the 'Cyrus Cylinder', referred to as history's first charter of human rights, where Cyrus sets out his decrees for a just society. A key element included racial and religious equality and the right of captives to be set free. Under this decree, the Israelites held in captivity in Babylon, were set free and from this time Jews around the world have upheld Cyrus as their liberator and remember him daily in their prayers.

Cyrus gained a great empire largely through diplomacy. He is remembered as a peacemaker and lawmaker and a model ruler He has been admired by leaders throughout history, including Napoleon and Alexander the Great, who is said to have visited his tomb.

Darius I earned the synonym 'the Great' for different reasons. He was a great military strategist and under his rule the Empire expanded to its furthest extent. Key to his success was his ability to build a navy. With the conquest of Egypt and the Levant, Darius acquired the best ship builders and sailors in the region.

The expansionist policies of the Achaemenids were checked when Darius invaded mainland Greece in 490 BCE. The Battle of Marathon could be seen as a watershed in the history of the West. The Persian defeat by a smaller force of Athenians marked the beginning of the end for the Achaemenids. It was not to be the end of the competition between the Greeks and Anatolians over the islands of the Aegean Sea, however. This is a tension that continues to this day, exemplified by the situation on the island of Cyprus that is divided between Greece and Turkey.

The Achaemenid Empire would come to an end in 330 BCE but its legacy would last for many centuries, if not millennia. Today many Iranians, for example, are rediscovering their rich heritage and are proud to share it with the world.

*****

CHAPTER THREE

Alexander the Great

Darius the Great was successful in conquering Thrace and subduing other Greek city-states largely because the Greeks were constantly at war with each other. This was to change with the rise of the hitherto unimportant kingdom of Macedonia under its king, Philip II.

Macedonia was situated in the mountainous region of northern Greece, bordering Thrace. Most Greeks viewed the country with contempt, considering the Macedonians to be uncouth barbarians. The only way to maintain any kind of peace between the different states and kingdoms of the Greek peninsula was through political or marriage alliances. Another way to ensure the loyalty of a vassal state was to hold royal children as hostages. This was the case with the young Philip II. When he was fourteen, he was sent as a hostage to Thebes, which at that time was the most powerful of the city-states.

Philip spent three years in Thebes, during which time he received diplomatic and military training from Epaminondas, one of Thebes' greatest generals and statesmen. But the most useful part of his training, which was to serve him well in later years, was a thorough grounding in Theban military tactics, especially that of the highly trained and well-disciplined *hoplites.* When Philip returned to Macedonia, he formed his own army using knowledge gained in Thebes. He introduced the use of the *phalanx,* which was a tight infantry formation, and also the 20-foot spear, known as the *sarissa.*

Philip's burning ambition was to invade and conquer Persia, the power that had held so many Greek cities in Asia Minor and along the Aegean coast, in subjugation under the rule of the *tyrants*. But before he could contemplate an invasion of the Achaemenid Empire, he had first to win the loyalty of the Greek city-states. Crucially, he needed the support of the Athenian navy and Thessalonian cavalry as well as Greek *hoplite* infantry.

Although the great Athenian orator Demosthenes warned the Greeks repeatedly of a Macedonian threat, he was ignored. They continued to believe that the Macedonians were a barbaric, backward race. It came as a surprise therefore that by 338 BCE, through a combination of diplomacy and at times force, Philip had secured the allegiance of most city-states, including that of Athens. Furthermore, he succeeded in founding the League of Corinth. Members of the League, all of whom committed troops to Philip's cause, included Corinth, Athens, Delphi, Olympia and Pydna, which was located in the region of today's Pieria. He also stationed Macedonian garrisons in each member state. Only Sparta refused to join the League, declaring that no Spartan could ever fight under the leadership of a barbarian.

Having united the city-states under his rule, Philip felt it was now time to prepare for his invasion of the Achaemenid Empire. He was further encouraged by reports of the Empire's weakness that he received from Persian exiles living in Macedonia. In 336, he sent a force of 10,000 men across the Hellespont from Europe into Asia so that they could prepare the way for the main Macedonian army.

Philip's last act before leading the invasion of Asia, was to organise a great ceremonial event that would include athletic games, sacrifices to the gods and sumptuous banquets. He invited dignitaries and ambassadors from all parts of the Greek Peninsula. When the King entered the theatre wearing a brilliant white robe, the crowds rose to their feet with roars of adoration. At that moment, a young royal body guard stepped forward, pulled a dagger from his cloak and thrust it into the King's heart.

The murderer was Pausanias. The motive is less clear. It was normal in the ancient world for the aristocracy to have young male lovers. Pausanias was an ex-lover of Philip and one theory is that he murdered the king in a fit of jealous rage. Another theory is that Pausanias was commissioned by Philip's wife Olympias, who had her own reasons for vengeance against the King. Even his own son, Alexander, was not immune from suspicion, since it is said that he was upset at not being included in the invasion party. Whatever the truth may be, Philip was now dead and the 20-year old Alexander succeeded as King of Macedonia.

The Young Alexander

Alexander III, known as the Great, was born in July 356, in Pella, Macedonia. His mother, Olympias, was Philip's fourth wife. She belonged to a snake-worshipping cult of Dionysus and according to Greek historians, she fell out of favour with Philip when he suspected her of sleeping with snakes. When Philip took another wife, Olympias and the young Alexander, went into exile, only returning to Pella on the eve of Philip's planned invasion of Persia. The Macedonian King had recalled Alexander and his mother to Pella because he wanted to leave his kingdom in the hands of his son and heir while he was on campaign. It should be mentioned that Alexander had a very close relationship with his mother that continued throughout his life.

The main source for the life of Alexander is the Greek historian Lucius Flavius Arrianus, better known as Arrian, who was born around 90 CE at Nicomedia. At that time, Nicomedia was the capital of the Roman Province of Bithynia and because he came from a distinguished family, Arrian had received Roman citizenship. He served on the Danube before becoming Governor of Cappadocia. Having studied the works of both Herodotus and Xenophon, he was fascinated by the life of Alexander the Great and after his retirement he wrote a monumental work entitled *The Campaigns of Alexander.*

As a young boy, Alexander was sent by his father to study under the great philosopher Aristotle. Aristotle had studied under Plato, who in turn had been a student of Socrates. Consequently, Alexander had imbibed the best of Greek thought. He studied medicine and science and he particularly enjoyed poetry. His knowledge of medicine would later be put to practical use when on the battle-field. His closest fellow students would remain friends for life and many of them joined him on his campaigns across the Levant to Egypt and eastwards across Central Asia to the Indus valley. Of these friends, he was particularly close to

Hephaestion and when his friend died at the age of 32, Alexander was distraught.

A well-recorded event surrounding the young Alexander, is the story of Bucephalus the horse. According to Plutarch, in around 344, a Thessalonian horse-trader offered Philip of Macedonia an enormous black horse that had a white mark on its massive head. Philip rejected the horse on the grounds that the price was too high and also because no-one had managed to tame it. But the 12-year old Alexander stepped forward, claiming that he would be able to tame it and that he would pay for the horse if he failed. After observing Bucephalus for a while, he realised that the animal became uncontrollable when it had its back to the sun, probably because the animal was afraid of its own shadow. So, he took the reins and gently walked the horse around to face the sun. With no fear of its shadow, Bucephalus became calm enough to mount.

Plutarch wrote that the proud Philip declared: *'O my son, look thee out a kingdom equal to and worthy of thyself, for Macedonia is too little for thee'.* Bucephalus was to remain by Alexander's side for the next eighteen years. He died in the Punjab in 326, after the Battle of Hydaspes,, either through old age or from battle injuries; most probably a combination of both.

Alexander, King of Macedonia

When Philip was assassinated in 336, Alexander immediately succeeded as King of Macedonia as well as Military Governor, or Commander-in-Chief of the League of Corinth. But ambitious as he was to follow in his father's footsteps and invade the Achaemenid Empire, he decided that the time was not yet right. Predicting that there might be some resistance to his rule from some city-states on the grounds of his youth, he believed that he must first secure their support before venturing into Asia.

His first task was to gain the loyalty of the army. It was at this point that Alexander's genius as a leader of men started to become apparent. Using the skills of oratory that he learned under Aristotle, he delivered a powerful speech that won the loyalty and admiration of his troops. He then purged the ranks of those known to have Persian sympathies. And despite the fact that he would have liked to get rid of some of his father's older generals, he wisely held on to the most experienced and able, the most important being Parmenion. He also invited some of his student friends to join his inner circle, appointing them to senior positions in the military and later as governors or *satraps* of his Empire.

By 334, Alexander had succeeded in gaining the allegiance of all the city-states apart from Sparta and he had once more subdued the rebellious Thracians. He was now ready to resume his father's task of conquering Persia. With almost 50,000 infantry, 6,000 cavalry and over 100 ships, he crossed the Hellespont into Asia unopposed. According to Greek tradition, Alexander was a descendent of Achilles, hero of the Trojan War. Consequently, when he landed on Persian soil he immediately made for Troy to pay homage to his great hero.

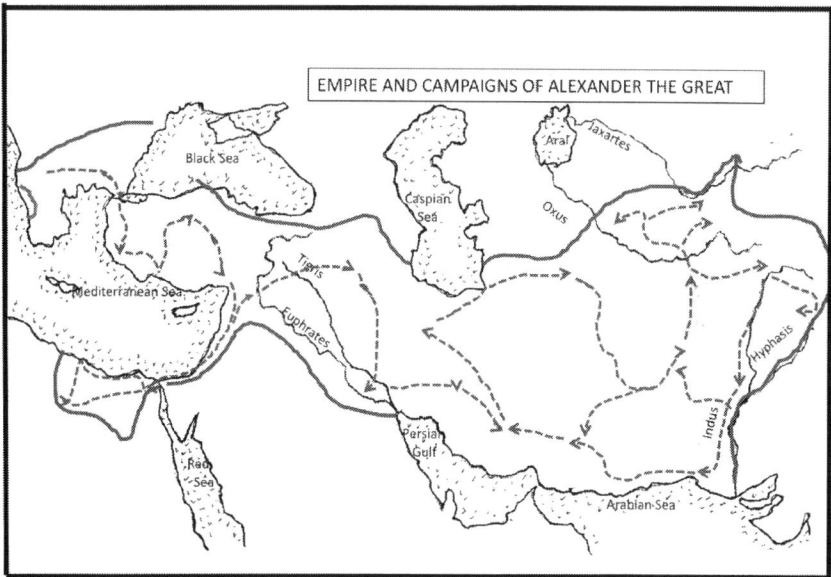

EMPIRE AND CAMPAIGNS OF ALEXANDER THE GREAT

The Battle of Granicus: May 334 BCE

Although the Persians knew of the Greek invasion and Alexander's movements, they were confident that they could force the Macedonians back across the Hellespont. Under the leadership of the *satrap* of Hellespontine Phrygia, the Persian troops, including units from distant parts of the Empire, positioned themselves at Granicus River (modern Biga River), which is in the Turkish Province of Canakkale. The Persians hoped that the narrow river would force Alexander's phalanx units to break formation.

According to Arrian, the Battle of Granicus began on the third of May. Parmenion, Alexander's second-in-command, advised that he should move upstream and attack the following morning. But the young king was impatient for action. In what became a characteristic of Alexander's battle tactics, he chose the element of surprise and attempted what many would think to be the impossible. His light infantry feigned an attack and while the Persians were occupied in pushing them back, Alexander swept forward at the head of a wedge-shaped cavalry charge, breaking through the Persian lines. Then, when it came to hand-to-hand fighting, the long Macedonian *sarissa* was far superior to the Persian javelin. The Greeks were victorious at Granicus. It was to be the first of three major battles during Alexander's conquest of the Persian Empire.

Greek casualties were said to be between 300-400, with Persian losses amounting to around 1,000 to 3,000. Alexander ordered the burial of the Persian commanders as well as his own troops. But he dealt harshly with those Greek mercenaries who had been fighting for the Persians. Out of some 18,000, half were executed. The remainder were sent to Macedonia to work as slaves. Hundreds of Persian sets of armour were sent to the Acropolis in Athens for display, bearing the inscription: *'Alexander, son of Philip and all the Greeks except the Lacedaemonians, presents this offering from the spoils taken from the barbarians inhabiting Asia'.*

Alexander then appointed a Macedonian General named Calas as *satrap* of Hellespontine Phrygia, with instructions that tribute from his new subjects should remain at the same level as under

Darius III. This was a pattern that he was to repeat throughout his period of conquest. From the start, his aim was to gain the loyalty of his subjects, to be seen as a just ruler and not a brutal conqueror. The exception to this was in his dealings with those who refused to submit to his rule, those who were disloyal, and above all, Greek mercenaries fighting on the side of the Persians.

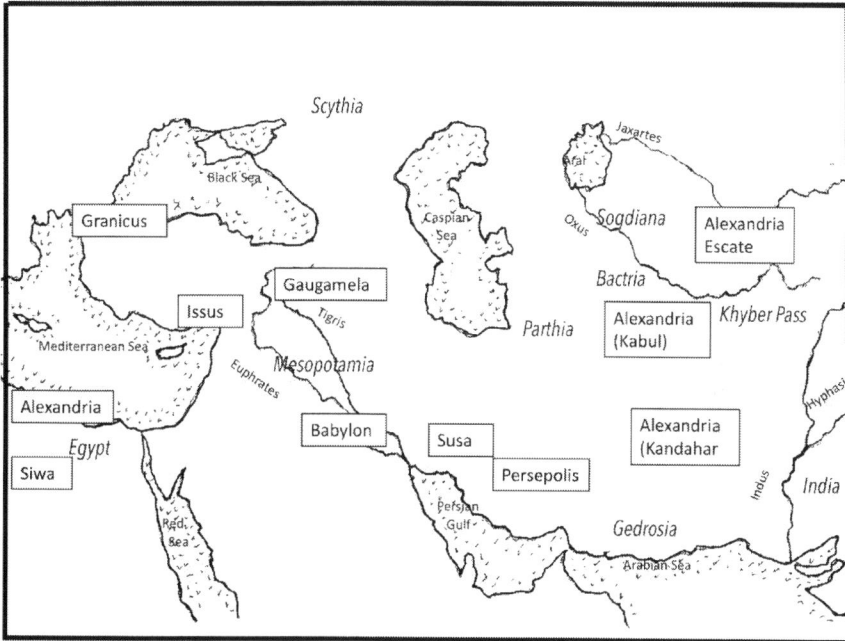

Scythia
Jaxartes
Black Sea
Granicus
Caspian Sea
Oxus
Sogdiana
Aral
Alexandria Escate
Gaugamela
Bactria
Issus
Tigris
Parthia
Alexandria (Kabul)
Khyber Pass
Mediterranean Sea
Euphrates
Mesopotamia
Alexandria
Babylon
Susa
Alexandria (Kandahar
Hyphasis
Egypt
Siwa
Persepolis
Indus
India
Red Sea
Persian Gulf
Gedrosia
Arabian Sea

The Battle of Issus: November 333 BCE

Although Alexander had beaten the Persians at Granicus, he knew that he could never claim sovereignty over the Persian Empire until he had eliminated the King of Kings. His first instinct was to follow him into the interior of Asia Minor, but this would leave the Anatolian coast vulnerable to attack from the Persian navy. He decided therefore that his first priority must be to secure the coastal cities of the Eastern Mediterranean before dealing with Darius.

When he reached the port of Halicarnassus, modern-day Bodrum, he was confronted by the Persian navy under the command of Memnon of Rhodes. Memnon was a Greek commander who had long been in the service of the Persians. He had fought against Philip of Macedon and he urged the Greek city-states to rebel against the Macedonians. During the siege of Halicarnassus, Alexander almost suffered his first setback at the hands of Memnon.

He was aided during the siege by Ada, the deposed Queen of Halicarnassus, who was living in the nearby fort of Alinda. After defeating Memnon, Alexander made Ada Queen of the territory of Caria, an area south of Ephesus. Ada and Alexander developed a close relationship and she adopted him as her son. It was a characteristic of Alexander's personality that during his short life he had good relationships with older women; the relationship with his own mother being a prime example.

From Halicarnassus Alexander travelled inland to the city of Gordium in order to meet up with fresh troops arriving from Macedonia. According to tradition, this was the location of the 'Gordian Knot' legend. Apparently, a local oracle had declared that the person who could undo a complicated knot, that secured an ox-cart to a post, would become ruler of Asia. Alexander succeeded where others had failed. One account says that he removed a pin, another that he simply cut it with his sword.

Following the Persian defeat at Granicus, Darius started to gather troops from across his Empire in preparation for an attack on the Macedonians. It took over a year for armies to arrive from as far away as the Indus Valley. Apart from troops, the Persian armies were accompanied by cooks, physicians and priests, plus wives and concubines, which was the custom of the Achaemenids when on campaign.

This time Darius personally led his troops from the front and he chose the location for battle. He decided on the ancient town of Issus, today's Iskenderun (Alexandria) in Southern Anatolia. Being located on a river and close to the Gulf of Issus, he hoped to gain a strategic advantage over the Macedonians. However, just as at Granicus, Alexander surprised the Persians and against all odds he was victorious.

The moment when the Macedonian King and the Achaemenid King of Kings came face to face in battle, is immortalised in the famous *Alexander Mosaic* which is now held in the National Archaeological Museum in Naples. It shows a mounted, bare-headed, Alexander confronting Darius who is riding his war chariot. The expression on Darius's face is a mix of surprise and terror. He fled the scene, leaving his wife and family behind. However, when Alexander later discovered his family, he treated them with kindness. Whether this was because Alexander had a propensity for kindness, especially towards women and children, or whether he was acting from political expediency, is arguable. After burying those who died in the battle, he then personally tended to the wounds of his injured soldiers using the knowledge he had gained while studying under Aristotle. It was this sort of action that won him the loyalty and admiration of his men.

The city of Issus was close to the wealthy trading centre of Damascus and although Alexander was tempted to take the city himself, he could not afford the time. He needed to press on down the coast of the Levant. He therefore sent his generals to secure the submission of the city. Many high-ranking Persians had taken refuge in Damascus and on hearing of the defeat at Issus and the close proximity of the Macedonians, they left the city, with as many of their treasures as they could carry. Unfortunately, they were captured on the road by Alexander's emissaries.

Among the refugees was Barsine, widow of Alexander's great enemy Memnon of Rhodes. In customary fashion, she was treated well. Furthermore, the Macedonian king was attracted to her. Although they never married, they had a long relationship and she bore him his first son, named Heracles.

With the surrender of the city of Damascus and the treasure captured from the refugees, Alexander now had enough money to pay his troops and continue his campaign of conquest. He also commissioned his first silver coin. With the head of young Hercules on one side and Zeus on the other, the coin symbolised the coming together of the Greek and the Oriental, which was to be a major theme throughout his reign.

Egypt

Alexander had been fascinated with Egypt from the time when he was a student under Aristotle as a boy. He held a lifelong desire to see the land and particularly to visit the oracle of Amun, which was deep in the Libyan desert. Before reaching Egypt, however, he had to subdue the coastal towns of the Levant, then known as Phoenicia.

The first city he encountered, which immediately surrendered, was Byblos in today's Lebanon. It is said to be one of the oldest continually inhabited cities in the world and is associated with the importation of papyrus from Egypt. *Biblos* was the Greek word for 'book', from which we get the word Bible. The next city to surrender, further along the coast, was Sidon.

In January 332, Alexander reached Tyre, which was the most important Phoenician city-state at the time. But here he faced fierce opposition. The city itself was located on an island, which was then about a kilometre from land and was protected by 150 ft walls and two natural harbours. After laying siege from his ships for seven months, to no effect, Alexander chose another tactic. He ordered the building of a causeway, large enough to withstand his siege engines, connecting the island with the mainland. When Tyre finally fell, the Macedonian king was unforgiving. According to Arrian, 8,000 inhabitants were massacred, among whom 2,000 were crucified. Those who took refuge in the Temple of Hercules were spared but 30,000, including women and children, were sold into slavery. Tyre was then burned to the ground. The causeway, which over time has silted up, remains to this day.

Alexander then moved on to Gaza, an important trading post between Egypt and Mesopotamia. The city was located on a hilltop and was protected by high walls. As with Tyre, the inhabitants refused to surrender. When the Macedonian siege engines were unable to reach the height of the walls, Alexander ordered his troops to construct a mound around the city, from which his siege-engines were able to attack the walls. The Gazans fought to the death but their leader survived. He was cruelly put to death by being tied to a chariot and driven around the city until he died.

The Macedonians had destroyed the city of Tyre but they wanted to keep its valuable trade connections. Consequently, they needed a new coastal port. Alexander discovered the ideal location further down the coast in Egypt. It was to be the first of some twenty cities located across his Empire that were to be named Alexandria. His vision for this first city was that it would become as great as Athens. He took a personal interest in its street planning, temple building and irrigation projects. Above all, he wanted it to be a cosmopolitan city, attracting the finest minds and greatest scholars. Some fifty years later, Alexandria would be home to the greatest library in the ancient world.

Having founded the new city, Alexander and his closest companions, made an unexpected journey deep into the Libyan desert. Their destination was the Oracle of Amun at the oasis of Siwa. In common with most Greeks of the time, Alexander believed that his life was controlled by the gods and the way to communicate with the gods was through an oracle. On this occasion, he wanted to know if it was Amun's wish that he should become ruler of the Persian Empire, to which the oracle replied, yes. According to the historians, he also asked the oracle if Philip was his real father. The reason for asking was because his mother had intimated that she had been impregnated by Zeus, probably by means of the snakes that she is said to have slept with. Apparently, the oracle answered that this was true. Consequently, Alexander believed himself to be the son of the god Zeus and also Pharaoh of Egypt.

Mesopotamia

In 331, Alexander left Egypt and turned eastwards towards Mesopotamia to continue his search for Darius. In early October, the two great kings met up again at the Gaugamela, near Erbil in modern Iraqi Kurdistan. Although faced by an army almost twice the size of the Macedonians, Alexander was successful in outwitting the Persians. Once more, Darius fled the scene and his troops retreated in disarray. It was the third and last major battle between the Macedonians and Persians.

Following the Battle of Gaugamela, Alexander made for the ancient city of Babylon (modern day Iraq), which surrendered, just as it had some two hundred years earlier to Cyrus the Great. While in Babylon, the King was fascinated by a black liquid bubbling through the desert sands which the people apparently used to seal their boats. But of more importance at the time, was the amount of treasure that he could squeeze out of the city. Apart from the constant need to pay his army, he also regularly sent money and treasures back to Athens to reassure the Greeks of his successful campaigns in order to maintain their loyalty.

Alexander then travelled to Susa, which was located in the Zagros mountains in today's Iranian province of Khuzestan. The city was reputed to be the location of the prophet Daniel's tomb. In Biblical tradition, Daniel had been captured by King Nebuchadnezzar at the time of the Babylonian Exile. (see Chapter Two). Many Central Asian people believe that the conquest of Alexander the Great was prophesied by Daniel. They identify Alexander as the 'fourth beast who would rise from the sea with ten horns, devouring the whole earth' (Daniel 7). Interestingly, Michael Woods, in his documentary *In the Footsteps of Alexander the Great* (BBC 1998), met villagers across today's Iran and Iraq who still tell the tale of the evil Alexander with 'two horns', who had invaded their country.

Susa was one of the wealthiest cities of the Achaemenid Empire. The city immediately surrendered and the *satrap* offered the Macedonian king enough gold and silver bullion to pay his troops for several years. Alexander stayed in the royal palace and at last achieved his ambition; to sit on the Persian throne. But he was a short man and his feet would not reach the floor.

When a table was placed under his feet, an elderly courtier became distressed and when Alexander asked the reason, he was told that the Persian King of Kings used to eat off the table. Alexander's immediate response was to remove it, but one of his generals intervened, telling him that this was a good omen; the table of his enemy had now become his footstool. The footstool is a powerful symbol of submission in the Near East and Central Asia. Centuries later, Alp Aslan, Sultan of the Seljuk Empire, was to humiliate the Byzantine Emperor, Romanos IV Diogenes, by famously using him as his 'footstool' after the Byzantines were defeated at the Battle of Manzikert in 1071 CE.

As mentioned earlier, when Darius fled the Battle of Issus in November 333, he left behind his wife and children. Consequently, they accompanied Alexander on the arduous journey to Egypt and back. Darius's wife, Stateira, died on the return journey. However, before leaving Susa in 330, Alexander resettled the family in their previous home. He particularly wanted to ensure that Sisygambis, the mother of Darius, was comfortable. Six years later, in 324, he married Darius's daughter, also named Stateira, at what is known as the Susa weddings. He also wanted his generals to follow his example and take Persian wives as a way of helping to integrate Persians and Greeks. A mass wedding took place according to Persian custom. Although most of the marriages were short-lived, it was sufficient time to produce a generation of Greek/Persian children.

Persepolis

Alexander then moved on to Persepolis which was the administrative, diplomatic and ceremonial centre of the Achaemenid empire. The only route to the city was through the narrow mountain pass known as the Persian Gates, which was guarded by the fearsome Uxian tribe. When the Uxians attacked the Macedonian army, Alexander was brutal in his retaliation and they were only spared annihilation through the intercession of Sisygambis, Darius's mother, who appealed to the King to spare the tribe.

With the defeat of Darius at Gaugamela and the surrender of Babylon, Susa and now Persepolis, Alexander's troops became restless, thinking it was time to go home. After sending the best of the treasures from Persepolis to Susa, he then allowed his soldiers to loot the city as a way of relieving their frustration.

The Macedonians were renowned for their heavy drinking and in the midst of the general revelry and rampage, the city caught fire and burned to the ground. There has been much debate as to whether this was purely accidental or perhaps intentional, possibly in revenge for the earlier Persian burning of Athens. Arrian tells us that Alexander later regretted the destruction of such a magnificent city.

The troops were to be disappointed. They were not going home. At this point, although Darius had fled the battle at Gaugamela, he was still alive and Alexander believed that he could not legitimately succeed as King of Kings until the reigning King of Kings was dead, or *mat*, in the Persian language. According to Philip Freeman, in his book *Alexander the Great, 'shah mat'* (Shah dead) is the origin of the expression 'check mate'.

After a brief visit to the nearby city of Pasargadae to visit the tomb of Cyrus the Great, who Alexander greatly admired, he began preparation for the long march eastwards towards Bactria in search of Darius. It was at this point that his style of leadership began to change. He was no longer solely the leader of a conquering army, he was now also the ruler of a great empire.

The Empire of Alexander the Great

In order to ensure a smooth transition from Persian to Greek rule, Alexander left in place the administrative structure of the Achaemenid Empire and where possible kept the presiding Persian *satrap* in office. He then established military garrisons under the command of a Macedonian general. Apart from acquiring taxes, gold, treasures and often horses from his new vassals, he was able to increase his army with local recruits. Consequently, he could afford to send some of his Greek troops home, especially those he suspected of disloyalty. As with all kings at that time, the fear of assassination was ever present,

To the concern of his own troops, the King began recruiting Persians and other subject people into his army, not as foreign units, but as integral members of the army. He recruited promising young Persians, taught them Greek and trained them in Macedonian warfare. The Macedonian generals were not pleased, fearing that the Persians would, in time, take their place.

Alexander continued to use the efficient Persian postal system to carry messages across the Empire as well as frequent letters back to his mother in Pella. Most importantly, he needed to circulate news of his campaigns and victorious battles, as a means of propaganda and a warning to those who may be considering rebellion.

He began to surround himself with Persian courtiers and started to wear Persian clothes in the style of Darius. The final straw, which was fiercely resisted, was over the issue of *proskynesis,* or prostration. Alexander now wanted all his subjects, including the Greeks and Macedonians, to adopt the Persian form of prostration which entailed lying face down at the foot of the monarch. None of this was popular with the Macedonian troops, who were used to Alexander fighting alongside them in battle as an equal, facing the same dangers and even attending to their wounds.

Bactria

After the Battle of Gaugamela, Darius sought refuge in Bactria, a region that roughly covers today's Afghanistan, Tajikistan and Uzbekistan. In 330, Alexander and his troops set off in search of the King of Kings. But when Darius was finally caught up with, he was on the point of death, having been attacked by the Bactrian *satrap* Bessus and left to die in his chariot by the roadside. Alexander was shocked at such an ignominious end for so great a King. He arranged for the body to be returned to his family in Susa and the last of the Persian King of Kings was finally buried alongside his predecessors at the royal tombs in Pasargadae.

With the death of Darius, the troops again thought it was time to go home. But Alexander won them over by arguing that the *satrap* Bessus had claimed the title King of Kings and as long as he remained alive, he was a threat to Alexander and the Empire. Historians suggest that he had other reasons to press on towards the east. He believed that he was semi-divine, the son of Zeus and that the gods had predicted that he would rule the world.

According to his tutor Aristotle, India was a peninsula that jutted out into a great ocean that surrounded the known world. Therefore, if India marked the end of the world, Alexander had to conquer India.

But first he had to deal with Bessus. This proved to be relatively easy in the end because the local warlords, believing that they would be better served by siding with the new King, decided to hand Bessus over to Alexander, who immediately ordered his execution.

By 329, five years after crossing the Hellespont, Alexander had reached Kabul in the mountainous region of the Hindu Kush, where he established the garrison town known as Alexandria-in-the-Caucasus. In order to reach Bactria, he had to tackle the treacherous Khyber Pass, which was controlled by fierce tribes who demanded money from all who wanted to pass., Alexander's response was swift and brutal, as it had been when faced with the same situation at the Persian Gates in Mesopotamia.

His next challenge was to cross the River Oxus. The troops made rafts out of tents that were stuffed with straw. It then took five days to get the troops, horses and camp followers across the river. Once into Bactria Alexander was to face his fiercest opponent yet: the Sogdian warlord Spitamenes. The Persians had never completely subdued the warlike Bactrians and Sogdians. They also built seven garrison towns along the Oxus as protection against the even more hostile Scythians. In the face of Alexander's invading army, the Scythians allied with Spitamenes. But the Macedonian phalanx battle formation was no match against the guerrilla tactics adopted by the ancestors of today's Uzbeks.

In 328, the situation changed when Spitamenes was assassinated. Some sources claim that his generals killed him, others that his wife cut off his head. All agree, however, that his head was sent to Alexander as proof of his death and that the motive was that it was in everyone's interests to surrender to the Macedonian king. The daughter of Spitamenes, Apama, later married Seleucus I Nicator. He was one of Alexander's generals and he later founded the Seleucid Empire. (see Chapter Four)

Two significant events occurred while Alexander was in the region. It was here, during the celebrations marking the surrender of a Bactrian city, that Alexander probably fell in love with a woman for the first time. In common with many Greeks of the period who had male lovers, he had a special relationship with Hephaestion, his student friend and now a general in his army. He also had female lovers such as Barsine, widow of Memnon of Rhodes, who bore him a son, Heracles. And he would later marry Stateira, daughter of Darius III and Parysatis II, daughter of Artaxerxes III of Persia, both of which were political marriages and took place at the Susa Weddings. But Roxana, the daughter of a Bactrian noble, was different. For Alexander it was a marriage of love. Furthermore, the marriage sealed the conquest of Central Asia.

The other event showed the darker side of Alexander's personality. For centuries there had been a Greek presence in Persia. The majority were mercenaries fighting for the Achaemenid army. Some were merchants, but there were also Greeks who had once been taken hostage by the Persians. When Alexander reached Sogdiana, north of Bactria, he came across a small village of Greek-speaking people. Apparently, they had been deported from the Aegean coast by Xerxes the previous century. Their fellow Greeks had suspected them of collaborating with the Persians and for their own safety Xerxes transported them to far-off Sogdiana. When Alexander arrived in their village, they greeted him as their king. But he saw them as traitors who had sided with the Persians at a time when Persia was invading Athens. In anger and resentment at what he perceived as disloyalty, he massacred every man woman and child.

The Indus

The Persians had added the Indus Valley to their Empire as the twentieth *satrapy*, but the status was purely nominal. Nevertheless, as a Persian province, Alexander believed that as successor to Darius III, the province now belonged to him. But, his real aim was to conquer the whole of India, making him ruler of 'the world'.

As Alexander marched eastwards towards the Punjab, most cities, including Taxila in today's Pakistan surrendered. However, when he reached the River Hydaspes in July 326, he was faced by the formidable army of King Porus, who refused to surrender. The Macedonians defeated the King's forces but Alexander was so impressed by the personal strength and bravery of King Porus, that he allowed him to keep all his lands.

Sadly, Alexander's beloved horse, Bucephalous was injured in the battle and died soon afterwards. In commemoration, the King founded a city named Alexandria Bucephalous close to where the horse died, but the exact location is unknown.

Return to Babylon

It was now eight years since Alexander had crossed the Hellespont into Asia Minor. His armies were exhausted. Many had suffered injuries. Their uniforms were either in tatters or non-existent which meant they had to wear Persian clothing or whatever they could find. When Alexander attempted to rouse them for an invasion further into India the army finally rebelled. They would go no further.

Reluctantly, the King of Kings had to make plans to go home. He decided to divide his army into three, each taking a different route. Some were to return via the same overland route. A second army was to go by sea, down the Indus to the Indian Ocean and then westwards towards the Persian Gulf. The third group, comprising 50,000 troops and camp followers, were to be led by Alexander himself. They were to travel by land, from the mouth of the Indus, along the Gedrosia coast towards the Persian Gulf.

A primary task of the navy was to chart the coastline of the Arabian Sea with a view to establishing trading posts between Persia and India. It was intended that the navy and Alexander's land force would journey along the coast in parallel. The land force would provide water for the navy by digging wells at strategic points, and the ships would carry food and other supplies for the land army.

Unfortunately, the Macedonian fleet, being more familiar with the Mediterranean Sea, was unprepared for the trade winds and tidal flow of the Arabian Sea. Consequently, the navy got delayed and was never able to meet up with Alexander's land army. Arrian gives a detailed account of the King's gruelling journey across the Gedrosian desert, which was the poorest and most infertile region of the Persian Empire. Hundreds died of fatigue, heatstroke, hunger and thirst. When Alexander finally arrived at the outskirts of Persepolis, he was left with only half the number of his troops. Almost all the camp followers, women and children had been lost.

Final Days

After giving thanks to the gods for a safe return, the royal court moved to Ecbatana. Being high in the Zagros Mountains the city provided a cool respite from the heat of Babylon. Here Alexander and his troops were able to recover from their arduous journey and celebrate their victories. In the midst of the drunken revelries, Hephaestion, Alexander's lifelong lover and friend became ill with a fever. Despite the best efforts of the King's doctor, he died a few days later, at the age of 32 years. The distraught King ordered the execution, by crucifixion, of the doctor and he then retreated in mourning.

In June of the following year, while staying in Nebuchadnezzar's palace in Babylon, Alexander died following several days of fever. There has been great speculation that the cause of death was poisoning. But it is equally likely that he died as a result of the long-term abuse of his body. For nine years, he had pushed himself almost beyond endurance. His bones had been broken from countless battle injuries. He had suffered numerous episodes of malaria and dysentery. At just 32 years, he was totally exhausted. During his final hours, his soldiers filed past him, many in tears.

Alexander had no obvious successor. According to Arrian, his generals leaned over the dying King. They asked him "to whom do you leave your kingdom?" He responded "To the strongest.' And then he died.

Conclusion

Alexander the Great has come down through history as perhaps the most famous military tactician of all time. His greatest achievement was the conquest of the mighty Persian Empire. But what is probably sometimes overlooked, is the fact that this might not have been possible had he not inherited his father's army.

Philip II of Macedonia not only provided Alexander with the best of tuition, from the finest minds of Athens, but he also made sure that Alexander received a military training befitting the son of a King. More importantly, Philip had united the Greek city states and built up a powerful military force that included the Athenian navy and Thebian hoplites. So when Philip was unexpectedly assassinated on the eve of his invasion of Asia, Alexander inherited an efficient, well-trained military force.

Much has been written about Alexander's character, which was clearly complex. He was a religious man in the sense that he consulted the oracles and sacrificed to the gods. He probably had a large ego. For example, he asked the oracle at Siwa if he was the son of Zeus and also if he would conquer the world. Knowing that the Macedonian king had already defeated the Persians in two major battles and then stormed down the coast of the Levant, taking all in his path, it is not surprising that the Oracle said 'yes'. Of course, in ancient times, the boundary between the human and the divine was blurred, as was the case with many Roman Emperors.

Perhaps his 'divinity' gave Alexander a sense of invincibility that led him to attempt the impossible, whereas his bravery could also have been interpreted as foolhardy and reckless. On the other hand, he would never expect his men to risk their lives if he were not prepared to do the same. The problem was that he usually expected too much of them. They did not feel superhuman, as he might have done.

He was an extremely good leader of men and seemed to possess the gift of persuasion. On so many occasions he was able to convince his troops to go the extra mile, even in the face of great danger and when their bodies were exhausted.

On the battle field he showed great determination and an unwillingness to be defeated. When faced with what appeared to be the insurmountable, he ordered his engineers to build bridges of boats, create straw-filled floating tents and constructed causeways. He earned the love and respect of his men because he was prepared to stand alongside them in battle, to tend to their wounds and bury the dead, not only of the Macedonians but also the enemy.

The loyalty of his troops was first put to the test after his capture of Persepolis. He was already displaying signs of grandeur following his experience at Siwa when he received confirmation of his semi-divine status. But when he finally sat on the Persian throne and was in possession of the capital of the Achaemenid Empire, he began to behave like an Emperor. Not only did he begin to dress like a Persian and adopt Persian customs, but he expected his generals to do the same.

As a young man Alexander did not show much interest in women, preferring the company of men. When his greatest male lover, Hephaestion died, he was inconsolable. He was also extremely protective towards older women, his mother being a prime example. But he also became close to Ada, the deposed Queen of Halicarnassus, and he was especially kind to Sisygambis the mother of Darius. On the other hand, he could be cruel, unforgiving and brutal, even towards his fellow Greeks.

Alexander's legacy would remain for centuries to come; probably even to this day. There are numerous cities named after him, the most famous being Alexandria in Egypt. But his greatest legacy would be the subsequent spread of Hellenism that had such profound consequences throughout the Eastern Mediterranean, across Central Asia and as far as the Indus. At the same time, he is remembered as 'Alexander the Accursed' by many in Iran and Central Asia. Remembered as one of the world's greatest military tacticians, he was also a man with an extremely complex personality.

*****

CHAPTER FOUR

The Hellenistic World: 323 BCE – 10 BCE

With the death of Alexander, the Generals were faced with the problem of who should be his successor. Alexander's half-brother, Arrhidaeus, was not considered capable on account of a mental disability. The King's son, Heracles, was ruled out because his mother, Barsine, had been Alexander's mistress and not his wife. That left the unborn child of Roxane, Alexander's Bactrian wife.

According to the Roman historian, Quintus Curtius Rufus, Alexander had passed his finger-ring to Perdiccas, one of his Generals, just before his death. This was taken to mean that Alexander wanted Perdiccas to act as Regent for Arrhidaeus until the birth of his son with Roxane, should it be a boy. The child was indeed a boy. He was born in August, 323, just two months after the King's death. He was named Alexander IV of Macedon.

Arrhidaeus, being another son of Philip II, was named Philip III of Macedon, but he was purely a figurehead. Nevertheless, Olympias, Alexander's mother, considered him to be a threat to her grandson and so she had him assassinated on 25th December 317, while his wife was forced to commit suicide. Roxane was equally brutal. With the approval of Perdiccas, she organised the poisoning of Stateira and Parysatis, the two Persian wives that Alexander had married at Susa, either of whom could also have been carrying Alexander's child.

When Perdiccas married Alexander's sister, Cleopatra, he joined the royal dynasty, albeit through marriage. This put him in a position of power that angered the other generals. In around 321, another general, named Ptolemy, stole the body of Alexander and took it to Egypt. When Perdiccas marched on Egypt to recover the body, aggrieved generals, including Seleucus, who were jealous of Perdiccas's power, seized the moment to have him assassinated.

Upon the death of Perdiccas, Roxane and her son went to Pella in Macedonia to live under the protection of Olympias. However, ten years later they were both murdered by another General, Cassander, who then seized the throne of Macedon for himself. A short time later, Cassander then murdered Olympias, marking the end of the family line of Alexander the Great.

Wars of the Diadochi: 322-275 BCE

The Diadochi, or 'followers', is the collective term used to describe the various generals, companions, bodyguards and family members, who all tussled for power following Alexander's death. Among the generals, the task was made difficult by the fact that there was no ranking system in the Macedonian army. Instead, Alexander had operated with a 'pool' of generals, and officers were appointed according to the need and circumstance of the moment. Consequently, the generals could expect promotion at any time, regardless of 'rank'. Since Alexander had no direct heir to make these decisions, the Diadochi were left at a loss.

They soon split into two factions; one supporting Alexander's half-brother, Arrhidaeus, (Philip III) the other supporting his son, Alexander IV. A compromise was finally reached at a conference held at Babylon. Known as the Partition of Babylon, it was to be the first of several such conferences. It was decided that Craterus, an infantry and naval commander, should become Guardian of the Royal Family; Antiper, General of Greece and Perdiccas, Regent of the Empire. Six new *satraps* were appointed. Among them, Ptolemy was made *satrap* of Egypt, a title he held until 305, when he declared himself Pharaoh of an independent monarchy. The *satraps* in the East, including Bactria and Sogdiana, were left untouched, as was the Indian kingdom of Porus and the *satrapy* of Taxila in the Punjab.

With the assassination of Perdiccas in Egypt, another conference was held in 321, known as the Partition of Triparadisus. This time, Antiper became Regent in place of Perdiccas, and Seleucus, previously Commander of the Companions, was made *satrap* of Babylonia.

Between 322 and 275, a period of some 47 years, wars raged across Alexander's Empire as the Diadochi fought for power. In 311, following a conflict known as the Babylonian War, Seleucus succeeded in gaining control of the eastern part of the Empire as far as the Indus. However, in 305, his rule in the east was challenged by Chandragupta Maurya, founder of the Indian Maurya Empire. After two years of conflict, Seleucus was forced to submit. Under the terms of the peace agreement, vast swathes of land were ceded to the Indian Emperor. The status of inter-marriage between the Mauryans and Macedonians was also regularised and Seleucus offered his daughter in marriage to Chandragupta. In return, Seleucus received 500 war elephants as compensation. At the decisive Battle of Ipsus in Phryia, in 301, these elephants contributed to the victory of Seleucus and his allies Cassander and Lysimachus, over Antigonus I and his allies.

Although minor conflicts would continue until 275, the Battle of Ipsus marked the high point of the Wars of the Diodochi. None of the belligerents had thus far achieved their aim of uniting Alexander's Empire. Instead, it was divided into five separate kingdoms, each ruled by a monarch.

Hellenism

The term 'Hellenism' refers to the Greek cultural influence that survived throughout Alexander's empire long after his death. 'Hellenic', on the other hand is a geographical term describing the region of the Greek mainland and islands. The Hellenistic period began in 323, with the death of Alexander the Great. In the west, it lasted until 31 BCE when Egypt was conquered by Rome. In the east, Hellenism survived until around 10 BCE, when the Indo-Greek kingdom fell to the Indo-Scythians, an Iranian nomadic people who migrated southwards from the region of today's Russia and Mongolia.

Although Alexander's Empire did not survive his death, his legacy continued with the spread of Hellenism. Across his Empire, from Egypt to India, and beyond, Greek became the language of trade and commerce. Greek philosophical thought infiltrated other belief systems, particularly that of Judaism and

Christianity and evidence of Greek art and architecture has survived in the region of Afghanistan to this day.

While small Greek communities had existed across the Persian Empire for centuries, Alexander's conquests led to a huge influx of Greeks to the region. Greek immigrants, Greek culture and Greek ideas travelled along the ancient Achaemenid trade routes that connected garrison towns and cities. The garrisons were manned by Greeks. The cities that Alexander founded were administered by Greeks and this attracted even more Greek colonists. The people of these Hellenistic cities were entertained to Greek dramas and inspired by Greek oratory in Greek style theatres. Libraries containing the works of Greek philosophers such as Aristotle, were built for their edification. Having said all that, Greek cultural influence was confined to the elite and did not generally filter down to the common people, whose lives continued very much as before.

As recent as the 1960s, ruins of a Greek city were discovered at Al-Khanoum in Northern Afghanistan. Initially it was thought that this was Alexandria on the Oxus that had been founded by the Conqueror. Another theory is that it was built around 280 by the Seleucid Emperor Antiochus I Soter. Regardless of who built the city, it has all the hallmarks of a Hellenistic site, with a Greek theatre, gymnasium, temple and acropolis. According to John D Grainger, in his book *The Rise of the Seleukid Empire,* the site is unusual because there is little evidence of ordinary housing. Also, once the Greco-Macedonian population left, the city fell into ruin and was never again populated. Excavations on the site have been intermittent due to the recent Afghan wars and ongoing political instability, but a certain amount of research has been able to continue.

One of the most profound, and long-lasting influences of Hellenism was on the Christian Church. The first churches were founded around the Eastern Mediterranean at a time when Hellenism was at its height. The Hebrew Scriptures had already been translated into Greek by the time of Christ. Known as the Septuagint, it was this Greek version that was used by Christ and the Apostles. Subsequently, the New Testament and the writings of the early Church Fathers, were also written in *koine* Greek, which was a common form of Greek that was used throughout the Hellenistic world.

Apart from the Greek language, Greek philosophy influenced Christian thought. Both the concepts of the *Logos* and the belief in dualism (the separation of body and spirit) have their roots in Greek philosophy. Another example would be stoicism, which manifested itself in Christian martyrdom at times of Roman persecution. Despite this early Greek influence, orthodox Christian theology has survived, partly because deviancy has frequently been declared heretical and consequently suppressed, sometimes severely, by Church authorities.

Another example of Greek influence in the eastern region of Central Asia, is Greco-Buddhist art, which flourished for almost a thousand years following Alexander's death. Often referred to as Gandhara art, in reference to the region of Northern Pakistan where it flourished, it is a synthesis of Classical Greek culture with Buddhism.

A typical example would be statues of the Buddha in Greek style clothing, which is thought to be the first representation of the Buddha in human form. The Buddhas of Bamyan, in the Hazarjat region of central Afghanistan, would be an example. Unfortunately, these magnificent statues, one standing 174 feet high and the other 115 feet high, were blown up by the Taliban in March, 2001, because the Taliban believed them to be idols.

Finally, the discovery of coins right across Central Asia and into the Tarim Basin, are testimony to Greco-Macedonia presence. Still being unearthed, often from deep below desert sands, they provide information about the names of *satraps*, kings, provinces, and towns as well as dates.

The Seleucid Empire: 312 BCE – 63 BCE

Seleucus I Nicator was born in Europos, Northern Macedonia, in 358 BCE. His father, Antiochus, had been a general in Philip II's army and as a young man Seleucus was a page at the King's court. His mother was known as Laodice and Seleucus would later name several cities after his parents. According to legend, in similar vein to Alexander the Great, Antiochus had told his son that he was a son of the god Apollo.

Seleucus had fought alongside Alexander on his campaigns throughout the Macedonian conquest of the eastern Mediterranean, across Persia and on to the Indus. He was one of the many generals who married Persian wives at the Susa Weddings in 324. The Seleucids would later claim that Apama was the daughter of Darius III in an attempt to portray themselves as legitimate successors to the Achaemenids.

Unlike the majority of the Susa marriages, Seleucus's marriage to his Batrian wife was successful and they went on to have three children; the eldest, Antiochus I Soter (Saviour), would succeed as Basileus, or King, of the Seleucid Empire.

As mentioned above, at the Partition of Triparadisus in 321, Seleucus was made *satrap* of Babylon. By the end of the Wars of the Diadochi in 275, he was in possession of territory that stretched from Mesopotamia to the Indus. However, although he was now ruler of the largest portion of Alexander's Empire, because his kingdom was landlocked, he lacked warships, unlike Ptolemy in Egypt or Lysimachus in Asia Minor. Moreover, he did not have access to the Greek territories, which deprived him of a regular supply of hoplites for his army.

Although militarily weak, Seleucus was perhaps the most inventive of Alexander's successors. His chosen strategy for both expanding and defending his empire, was to found cities that would provide both taxation and manpower. As garrison towns, the cities served as a defence against invasion. Seleucus's first city, that was to be his capital and contained the royal tombs, was Seleukeia-on-Tigris, in the region of today's Baghdad. Seleukeia was later overshadowed by Antioch on the Orontes in Syria which was probably named after his father, Antiochus. Antioch also offered direct access to the Mediterranean.

A mix of Akkadian, Aramaic and Greek was spoken in most cities and an *ekklesia*, or assembly of citizens, was formed. Seleucus also appointed a 'central government', which was a court of men known as his *philoi,* or friends, who would perform duties such as governors, military commanders or royal advisers.

Following the peace agreement in 303 with Chandragupta Maurya, Seleucus left his eastern provinces in the hands of *satraps* and turned his attention to the West. His next aim was to conquer Thrace, Macedonia and Greece. With the exception of Ptolemy's Egypt, this would have made his empire equivalent to that of Alexander the Great. But this was not to be. He failed to bring the Greek territories under his rule. Soon after crossing the Hellespont, in September 281, he was assassinated by Ptolemy Keraunos, King of Macedon.

Antiochus I Soter: 281-261 BCE

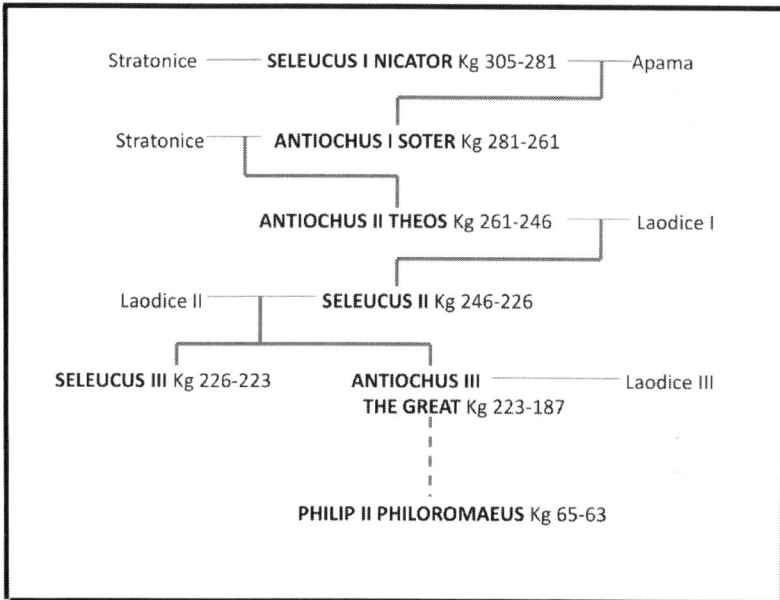

In order to concentrate on his invasion of Europe, Seleucus had put his son Antiochus in charge of the eastern provinces as their King. Around the same time, in December 281, Antiochus married his step-mother, Stratonice of Syria. Stratonice was just 17 when she had married Seleucus but despite the difference in age, she bore him a daughter. However, according to the historians, because Antiochus was infatuated with his young mother-in-law, Seleucus decided to permit the two to marry. They subsequently had five children, the eldest of whom was executed by his father for treason. The marriage of Stratonice and Antiochus has caught the imagination of many painters over the centuries, an example being *Antiochus and Stratonica* by the French painter Jacques-Louis David.

When Antiochus succeeded Seleucus, he abandoned his father's ambition to conquer Europe and he made peace with the Macedonian King. At the same time, he gave up any idea of taking Bithynia or Anatolia, largely because he had to deal with rebellions in Syria.

His greatest challenge came in 278 when the Gauls, (Celtic clans) who had settled in the Balkans, invaded Seleucid territory. Antiochus succeeded in pushing the Gauls back in 275 by employing his war elephants. Subsequently viewed as 'saviour' of the Seleucid Empire, he earned the title 'Soter' (Saviour). Although the Gauls had been halted, they were not defeated and in time they settled in the region of Anatolia that became known as Galatia. The Galatians often fought as mercenaries for the Ptolemies of Egypt and later featured in the letters of St Paul that appear in the New Testament of the Christian Bible.

Syrian Wars: 274-168 BCE

Throughout history, the Mediterranean coast that incorporates today's Syria, Lebanon, Israel and Egypt has been fought over by competing powers. In ancient times, the coastal strip was known as Phoenicia and the region of the Beqaa Valley, between Mount Lebanon and the Anti-Lebanon Mountains was referred to as Coele-Syria.

Following the Battle of Ipsus between the Diadochi in 301, Ptolemy I of Egypt occupied the region, despite the fact that Seleucus had been awarded Coele-Syria under the peace treaty. Even though Seleucus needed access to the Mediterranean, he did not challenge Ptolemy, probably because the latter had frequently supported him in earlier conflicts. But this all changed with the deaths of these two leaders. Their successors, Ptolemy

II Philadelphus and Antiochus I, came into conflict over possession of the region.

Between 274 and 168, the Ptolemies and the Seleucids fought six wars, during which time cities constantly changed hands, a situation that led to growing instability. At the same time, the Roman Republic was gaining influence in the Mediterranean. Rome depended upon grain from North Africa to feed its citizens and the Republic was getting increasingly anxious that her grain supplies from Egypt would be disrupted if the Syrian Wars continued. Consequently, Rome supported the Ptolemies against the Seleucids; a situation that contributed to a closer relationship between Egypt and Rome that would eventually result in Rome's annexation of the country.

In the context of growing instability, nationalism grew in both Egypt and Coele-Syria. Egyptians called for the overthrow of their Greek Ptolemaic rulers and the Judaean Jews wanted freedom from the Seleucids on the grounds that Hellenism was a threat to their religious way of life. The First Book of Maccabees in the Bible describes how Simon Maccabeus succeeded in defeating the Seleucids in 168. The Hasmonean dynasty was then founded and was to last until 37 BCE, when Herod the Great was made king of the Roman client kingdom of Judaea. Seven years later, in 30 BCE, Egypt finally fell to Rome following the defeat of Cleopatra VII, the last Ptolemaic Pharaoh, and her ally the Roman General Mark Anthony, at the Battle of Actium.

Greco-Bactrian Kingdom: 256-125 BCE

Seleucus and his successors were forced to spend most of their time defending their western provinces, initially against the Ptolemies and later against the rising power of Rome. Consequently, the Hellenistic provinces in the East were left in the care of *satraps* who governed with increasing autonomy.

Although source material is limited compared to the western provinces, Strabo, the Greek geographer and historian, who lived in Asia Minor between 63 BCE and 24 CE, provides some information about Bactria. Chinese sources include the Book of Han and the Histories of Chinese court historian Sima Qian.

Historians of the Indian Maurya Empire, as well as Buddhist texts, also refer to the Greeks (Yavanas) of Central Asia.

Opinions differ as to exactly when Diodotus, the *satrap* of Bactria seceded from the Seleucid Empire. Likely dates are sometime between 250 and 247, at a time when the Syrian Wars were at their height. The year 247 would coincide with the fall of the Seleucid capital, Antioch on the Orontes, to the Ptolemies, to be quickly followed by the assassination of the Seleucid King Antiochus II. Consequently, the Seleucids found themselves in a power vacuum which Diodotus was quick to take advantage of. Since the Seleucids were in no position to respond to Diodotus's act of secession, he was left unchallenged, at least for the moment.

Diodotus became King of an independent Greco-Bactrian kingdom that incorporated the fertile region of Bactria, as well as Sogdiana. He was known as Diodotus I Soter, taking the epithet Soter ('the Saviour') on the grounds that he had liberated his kingdom from Seleucid rule. At about the same time, Andragorus, *Satrap* of Parthia, proclaimed independence from the Seleucids. But with no military support to defend his northern border, he was soon overthrown by Arsaces, leader of the Parni Tribe, who would then go on to found the Parthian Empire. (See Chapter Five)

Antiochus III came to the Seleucid throne in 222 BCE and ruled for 36 years. He earned the epithet 'the Great' because he was able to restore Seleucid rule to territory previously taken by the Ptolemies and also because of his campaigns in the eastern provinces and India. In 209, the Seleucid king attempted to retake Bactria from King Euthydemus I, who was then king of Bactria. After a two -year siege of the Bactrian capital city of Balkh, the Seleucids withdrew. Under the terms of the peace agreement, the independent Kingdom of Greco-Bactria was recognised and the hand of Antiochus's daughter was offered to the son of Euthydemus. Antiochus then travelled to Kabul, which at the time was ruled by the Indian King Sophagasenus, who gave him more war elephants before he returned to the West.

From this point, the Greco-Bactrian Kingdom expanded eastwards, beyond the city of Alexandria Eschate (the furthest), that had been founded by Alexander the Great and into the region of Xinjiang, modern day China. It would appear that relations between China and Greco-Bactria were good. The Book of Han speaks of wealthy urban cities that were equal to any in China. More importantly, a regular trade relationship developed between Chinese and Bactrian cities that marked the beginning of what became known as the Silk Road. For example, Sima Qian records how Zhang Qian, imperial diplomat to Emperor Wu, discovered many Chinese goods being sold in the markets of Bactria.

Archaeological evidence reveals Greek influence in various forms of Chinese art. Apart from Greek motifs on pottery and coins, Chinese statues depict warriors that mirror those of Greek classical culture. This raises the possibility that Greek artists might have been employed by Chinese courts. It has even been suggested that Greeks might have worked on the famous Terracotta Warriors in Emperor Qin's tomb (247-221 BCE), but this is refuted by today's Chinese.

Indo-Greek Kingdom: 180 BCE-10 CE

From the time of the peace treaty between Seleucus I and Chandragupta Maurya in 303 BCE, a Greek ambassador attended the Mauryan court at its capital city of Pataliputra (modern-day Patna in the Indian state of Bihar). The Greek historian Megasthenes was one of the first ambassadors to the Indian court and he gave a detailed description of the city in his book *Indika.* In 1895, archaeologists discovered a large rectangular capital in the ruins of the royal palace. Known as the Pataliputra Capital, it is decorated with Hellenistic style motifs, suggesting a strong Greek influence and perhaps even the work of Greek artisans.

Relations between the Indians and Greeks were further strengthened during the reign of Chandragupta's grandson Emperor Ashoka (reigned 268-232 BCE). According to tradition, Ashoka converted to Buddhism following the brutal war against the Kalinga (modern Odisha in Eastern India). Overcome by the deaths, deportations and destruction of the war, Ashoka is said to have had a religious experience that resulted in his conversion.

From this point on, he promoted the spread of Buddhism not only across the Indian sub-continent, but as far west as Ptolemaic Egypt. His famous 'Edicts of Ashoka', which were inscriptions written on pillars, stones and cave walls, were written in Greek and Aramaic as well as the Indian language of Prakrit. An extract from the Major Rock Edict No. 13, declares that the conquest by the *Dharma* (doctrine of the Buddha) was *'won where the king Antiochus reigns, and beyond where reign the four kings Ptolemy, Antigonos, Magas and Alexander'.* This quotation is clearly reference to the entire Hellenistic world. Furthermore, during this same period, many Greeks living in Bactria converted to Buddhism and Greek monks were known to have embarked upon missionary journeys in order to spread the *Dharma.*

When Ashoka died in 232, after a reign of 36 years, he was succeeded by a series of weak rulers. The last emperor, Brihadratha, was assassinated in 185 by his commander-in-chief, Pushyamitra Shunga, who then went on to found the Shunga Dynasty that lasted for approximately 100 years. According to Buddhist sources, Buddhism was severely persecuted by the Shunga, who were Hindu. The degree of persecution has been questioned by scholars, but whatever the truth may be, many Buddhists migrated at this time to Afghanistan and Bactria.

In 180, King Demetrius I of Bactria invaded India. It is possible that his motive was to protect the Greeks who were now living under the intolerant Shunga. However, his timing was fortuitous because since the fall of the Mauryan Empire, in 185, the Khyber Pass had been left unprotected. Demetrius is recognised as the founder of the Indo-Greek Kingdom, which was centred around several capitals, including Taxila and Sakala, both in today's Punjab.

The most famous of the Indo-Greek Kings was Menander I Soter (Milinda in Buddhist sources), who reigned between around 160-130 BCE. Apart from ruling the Punjab, he launched campaigns southwards into Rajasthan and eastwards towards the River Ganges. Although Menander was a great patron of Buddhism, other religions, including Hinduism and Jainism, thrived. When he died, portions of his ashes were enshrined in Buddhist stupas across his kingdom.

Decline

For centuries, the eastern provinces were in danger of attack from northern nomadic tribes. The Xiongu, who traditionally inhabited today's Mongolia, Siberia and northern China, were a particular threat. The Chinese built the Great Wall partly as a defence against the Xiongu. The Scythians, also known as Saka, who originated in a region north of the Black Sea, also made frequent raids into Central Asia.

Alexander the Great had built various garrisons along the northern border of his kingdom but when the Parthian and Bactrian *satrapies* seceded from the Seleucids, they lost Seleucid protection and became vulnerable to attack.

In 176, the Xiongu attacked the Yeuzhi tribes who lived in the Gansu province of today's northwest China. Consequently, the Yeuzhi split into two groups and fled their country. One group, known as the Greater Yeuzhi, migrated westwards, first into Sogdiana and then into Bactria where they conquered the Greco-Bactrian Kingdom. The Greeks then moved eastwards into India, marking the beginning of the Indo-Greek Kingdom.

The Chinese diplomat Zhang Qian visited Bactria in 126 at the time of Yuezhi rule. According to Sima Qian's *Records of the Grand Historian*, Zhang described the Yeuzhi as '*a nation of nomads, moving from place to place with their herds, and their customs are like those of the Xiongnu*'. He said that the men had deep-set eyes and heavy beards and that they were skilful at commerce. Interestingly, he also observed that women were held in great respect, to the point where men actually sought their advice before making decisions.

In around 80 BCE, soon after the death of the Indo-Greek King of the Hindu Kush, the Yeuzhi invaded and conquered the region. Further territories were lost to the Scythians in 46 BCE and in 10 BCE, the eastern Punjab, the last of the Hellenistic polities, fell. Although small communities of Greeks continued to live in the region throughout the 1st Century CE, the year 10 BCE marks the end of Hellenistic rule in the East. In the West, while Syria became a Roman Province in 64 BCE, the Battle of Actium, in 31 BCE, is the traditionally accepted date for the end of Hellenistic rule.

Conclusion

When Alexander the Great's empire was divided among his various generals, war was inevitable because each held a secret ambition to be the sole ruler of a reunited empire. Following the Wars of the Diodochi, Ptolemy and Seleucus emerged as the two most powerful leaders. Ptolemy ruled Egypt and parts of the Levant, while Seleucus held by far the largest territory which became the Seleucid Empire, stretching from Mesopotamia to the Indus.

Apart from Antioch on the Orontes, the empire was largely landlocked. This left the Seleucids militarily weak due to a lack of warships and a regular supply of hoplites from the Greek territories. Initially Seleucus planned an invasion of Macedonia and Greece but soon abandoned the idea. His alternative strategy was to consolidate power by founding cities that generated both taxation and manpower. It was these cities that formed the nuclei of Hellenistic culture. The cities were governed by Greeks and the elite enjoyed all the benefits of a Greek city comparable to those in their homeland, while the local populace lived much as before.

Because successive Seleucid kings were occupied in the West, defending their territory from the Ptolemies, the *satraps* of the eastern provinces ruled with relative freedom. It was only a matter of time therefore before signs of secession became apparent. Parthia made the first move, followed by Bactria.

When Antiochus III, the Great, failed to bring the Bactrians into line, the kingdom of Greco-Bactria became fully independent.

Without the support of the Seleucids, the eastern *satrapies* were vulnerable to attack from nomadic tribes from the North. When the Greco-Bactrian kingdom fell to the Yeuzhi, the Greeks moved eastwards into India and established the Indo-Greek Kingdom. Detailed records of these events are limited, but we get some idea of the chronology from the many coins that have been unearthed.

The Hellenistic period lasted for just over three hundred years. Culturally, it was a time of great creativity as the Greek language, arts and ideas synthesised with local traditions. This was especially the case in the eastern provinces where Buddhism flourished alongside Hellenism. In the West, Hellenism had an influence on Judaism and the early Church.

With the rise of the Parthians in the North, the Kushans in the East, and the Romans in the West, the kings of the Hellenistic world gradually fell from power. But Greek art, philosophy, literature, medicine, science and theatre were kept alive and have survived to this day.

*****

CHAPTER FIVE

Parthians, Kushans and Sassanids

Between the fall of the Seleucids in 63 BCE and the arrival of Islam in the 7th Century CE, Central Asia came under the rule of several major powers. The Parthians succeeded the Seleucids and eventually controlled an area including most of Central Asia and large parts of the Eastern Mediterranean. In 224 CE, the Parthians were overthrown by the Sassanids, who held power until conquered by Islam in 651 CE. Throughout most of this period, both the Parthians and Sassanids had to face the growing threat of Roman expansion, a situation that resulted in a state of almost constant warfare. In the East, the Kushans, a branch of the Yeuzhi, conquered the Indo-Bactrians and Indo-Scythians and established the Kushan Empire that ruled an area incorporating today's Afghanistan and the northern part of the Indian sub-continent, until 375 CE.

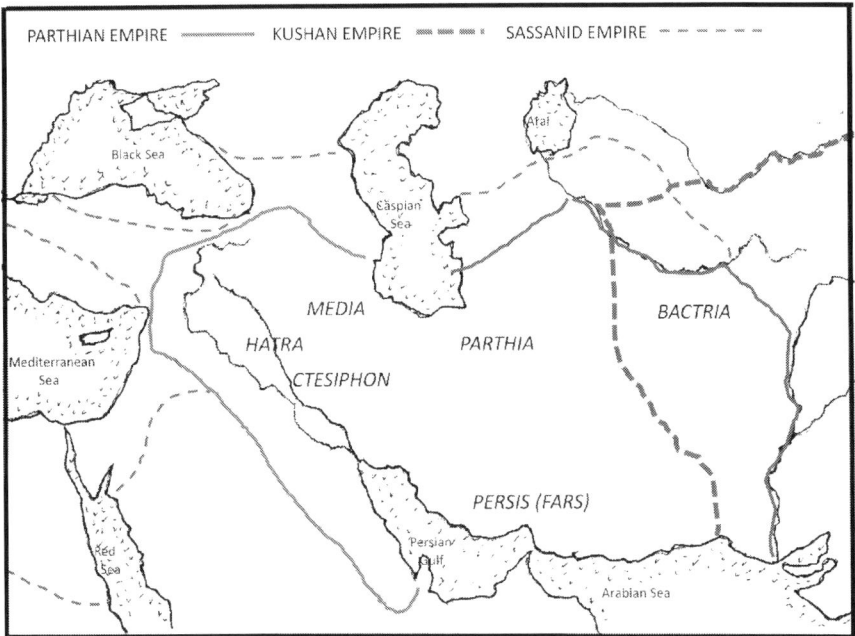

The Parthian Empire: 247 BCE-224 CE

The first Iranian mention of Parthia (Parthava) appears in the Behistun inscription of Darius the Great (see Chapter Two). The inscription mentions the region as one of the many territories conquered by Darius, which then became a *satrapy*, or province. Parthia later surrendered to Alexander the Great when he conquered the Achaemenid Empire.

As mentioned in the previous chapter, in 247 BCE, Andragorus, the *satrap* of Parthia, declared independence at a time when the Seleucids were preoccupied with the Syrian Wars. However, without Seleucid support to protect his northern border, Andragorus was quickly overrun by the Parni tribe of the Dahae confederation that inhabited an area roughly equating to modern Turkmenistan.

According to tradition, the chieftain of the Parni was Arsaces, who became the founder of the Parthian Empire. The Parthians were enemies of both the Seleucids and the Romans and so not surprisingly, Arsaces and his successors have been portrayed in a negative light by Greek and Roman historians. Some historians have even suggested that Arsaces was a legendary figure, and that the true founder of the dynasty was his brother Tiridates. However, this theory has been refuted by modern scholars and the more recent discovery of pottery and coins dating from the period, bearing the name of Arsaces, supports his legitimacy.

Soon after conquering Parthia, Arsaces seized the neighbouring *satrapy* of Hyrcania. He also founded the city of Asaak, which became the royal necropolis, as well as the cities of Dara and Nisa, where he began minting silver and bronze coins with both Persian and Greek influences. One side of these coins depicted Seleucid aristocracy, while the other side featured an Achaemenid king, often with a pointed cap and wearing Iranian riding clothes.

Arsaces died in 217 BCE, having ruled for thirty years. He is regarded as the 'Father of the Nation' and for two hundred years an ever-lasting fire, which is a feature of Zoroastrianism, burned in his honour in the city of Asaak. To this day, there are communities in the Caucasus and Armenia, that claim to be descendants of a branch of the Arsaces dynasty.

Although Arsaces and his immediate successors held the title King and ruled with considerable autonomy, minting coin and levying taxes, they still paid tribute to the Seleucids. However, this was to change under the rule of Mithridates I.

Mithridates I: 171-132 BCE

The name Mithridates means 'gift of Mithra', Mithra being a Zoroastrian divinity. Mithridates I (not to be confused with Mithridates VI of Pontus), succeeded his elder brother, Phraates I who died at a young age. Rather than nominate one of his young sons to rule, Phraates broke with tradition and named his younger brother, Mithridates, as his successor.

Because of his expansionist policies, Mithridates is sometimes referred to as 'the Great' and has also been favourably compared to Cyrus the Great. He was also the first Parthian king to adopt the ancient Achaemenid title of 'King of Kings'. After seizing Bactria in around 150 BCE, Mithridates then turned his attention towards the West with the aim of conquering Syria, so giving him access to the Mediterranean Sea. In 148, he successfully invaded the Seleucid territory of Media, followed by Babylonia in 141. But in 140, he was forced to abandon his plans for Syria in order to return to the East to deal with the Saka tribes who were attacking his eastern provinces.

Mithridates reintroduced Achaemenid, or Persian traditions, while keeping those of the Seleucid Greeks. Persian became the language of the court and Pahlavi was the official script. Coins, on the other hand, continued to be minted with inscriptions in Greek.

The court of Mithridates was peripatetic, moving from one city to another according to circumstances. Ctesiphon, on the Tigris, was the most important of the 'imperial' cities. Other cities included Seleucia, previously the capital city of the Seleucids and Ecbatana, the ancient capital of the Medes and summer residence of the Achaemenids. It had also been a favourite retreat for Alexander the Great when seeking respite from warfare. Nisa, in today's Turkmenistan, became the royal city of the Parthians in the East. Although the city was destroyed by an earthquake in the 1st Century BCE, archaeologists have subsequently unearthed numerous tombs, buildings and works of art from the site that date from the reign of the early Parthian kings.

By the time of his death, in 132 BCE, Mithridates I had transformed a small kingdom in northeast Central Asia, into a vast empire that controlled large segments of the Silk Road. He was succeeded by his son Phraates II, who ruled until 127, followed by the short reign of Artabanus I. In 124 BCE, Mithridates II, also known as the Great, came to the throne.

While Mithridates I adopted the Persian title, King of Kings, he was rarely referred to as such by his subjects. Mithridates II, on the other hand was universally acknowledged as King of Kings. One of his first tasks on succeeding to the throne, was the further consolidation of Parthian rule over Media and Babylonia, where he established several vassal states, including the kingdom of Armenia.

In around 120, Mithridates II received an envoy from the Han Chinese Emperor requesting that the Parthians form an alliance with the Chinese against their common enemy, the Xiongu. Although the Parthians turned down the request, the two powers agreed to strengthen trade relations along the Silk Road, so allowing silks, spices and horses to travel between China and Rome. Since much of the Silk Road passed through Parthian territory, the Parthians gained considerable wealth, largely through the collection of tolls.

The Roman Republic long held an ambition to conquer all the territory previously held by Alexander. This brought them into conflict with the Parthians. Consequently, Asia Minor became a battle-field between the Romans and the Persians. However, in 96 BCE, in the spirit of cordial relations, the Roman General Sulla and Mithridates II, agreed that a boundary be set between their two powers. The boundary became the River Euphrates and the city of Dura-Europos, in today's Syria, became an important border town and archaeological site. Unfortunately, many of its most valuable artefacts, including ancient churches and synagogues, were destroyed during the recent Syrian Civil War and were further looted by the Islamic State (ISIS).

Parthian Military

The Parthians had learned a great deal about tactics and military strategy from the Seleucids, the northern tribes and the Romans. They adopted what methods best suited them, while rejecting others. For example, they chose not to use war elephants as had been the practice of the Seleucids and instead concentrated on horses. Nor did they have a standing army. Instead they imposed a troop levy, often supplemented by mercenaries, on each of their eighteen vassal states, from which they also received tribute.

Parthian forces were almost entirely made up of cavalry, backed up by a small number of camels that were used to carry heavy baggage. They believed that infantry would be ineffective against nomads and the Roman phalanx. Light cavalry was employed for skirmishes and hit and run attacks, while heavy cavalry, or cataphracts, was used for close combat. The light cavalry wore limited armour to allow for greater flexibility. The heavy cavalry, sometimes referred to as the equine tank, wore steel helmets and heavy leather armour that was covered with metal plates. This protected the rider from head to knee. Horses were similarly protected. The Parthian armour later proved to be less effective against the lighter, more flexible, chainmail worn by the Romans. The normal weapon of the heavy cavalry was a lance and sword, while the light cavalry carried a double-curved bow that they had adopted from the Scythians.

By far the greatest asset of the Parthians was the horse that was bred in the Fergana Valley of today's Uzbekistan. Known as the Great Horse by the Parthians, and the Heavenly Horse by the Chinese, it is also referred to as the 'sweating blood' horse, probably due to a blood-sucking parasite that settled on the skin. The Parthian horse was even stronger and faster than the golden-coloured Akhal-Teke horse favoured by the Scythians. Above all, the Fergana horse was the perfect riding horse. The combination of this swift horse and its Parthian rider gave rise to the term 'the Parthian Shot', reflecting the ability of the mounted archer to ride at full speed, while shooting arrows backwards. It was a tactic frequently used when feigning retreat and required great skill at a time when there was no stirrup.

When the Chinese diplomat Zhang Qian visited Fergana in 103 BCE, he was so impressed by the Great Horse that he took a number back with him to the Chinese court. From this time on, these prized horses were traded between Central Asia and China. By the time of the Tang Dynasty (7th-8th Century CE), paintings of the Heavenly Horse were in great demand among the Chinese aristocracy. The Great Horse was frequently offered as a gift to Byzantine Emperors and it is said that Crusaders took them back to Europe during the crusading period of the 11th–13th Centuries.

The Kushan Empire: 30 CE-375 CE

While the Parthian Empire ruled in the Western regions of Central Asia, the Kushans came to power in the East. Known by the Romans and Greeks as the Indo-Scythians, the Kushans were one of the five branches of the Yuezhi nomadic confederation. Little was known about the Yuezhi until the 19th Century, when archaeologists discovered coins bearing the names and dates of various Kings that matched those of Chinese sources. More recently, the discovery of mummies in graves located in the Tarim Basin, dating back to the 2nd Century BCE, reveals that tall, Indo-European people once inhabited the region. DNA testing has further shown that these people had blond hair and flowing moustaches, unlike the East Asian people.

It is thought that the Yuezhi were forced to migrate southwards from the Tarim Basin into the Greco-Bactrian Kingdom in order to escape the nomadic Xiongnu tribes. Consequently, the Greeks of Bactria migrated across the Hindu Kush into India where they founded the Indo-Greek Kingdom. (See Chapter Four). In around 30 CE, the prince of the Yuezhi Guishuang (Kushan) tribe, named

Kujula Kadphises, defeated the other four Yuezhi tribes and became the first King of a united Kushan Dynasty.

At its peak, the Kushan Empire covered a region that stretched from the Aral Sea in the west, incorporating today's Uzbekistan, Afghanistan, Pakistan and large parts of northern India as far east as Benares. Its vast trade network allowed goods to be carried from the Indian Ocean, up the Indus Valley to join the Silk Road, from where merchandise then travelled westwards to Rome and eastwards to China. At the time, the Kushan Empire was a trade power equal to that of Rome and China.

The Kushans established several capital cities, including Begram, Peshawar and Taxila in today's Pakistan. Mathura in the Uttar Pradesh Province of India was the Kushan's winter capital. Their coins, while modelled on the Roman coins that were used along the Silk Road, were minted with the Greek alphabet. Another feature was that Kushan kings, showing artificially deformed skulls, were often portrayed on coins. Skull deformation was a common practice in Central Asian cultures at the time. Other coins were minted with Zoroastrian deities and gods of the Greek cults, Hinduism and Buddhism, which was testimony to the religious tolerance and diversity of the Kushans.

But it was Buddhism that received the greatest patronage, particularly during the reign of King Kanishka who ruled between 120-144 CE. Known as Kanishka the Great, he established his capital at Purusapura in Gandhara, today's Afghanistan. Kanishka is particularly remembered for convening the Fourth Buddhist Council at Kashmir.

An earlier Fourth Buddhist Council had taken place in Sri Lanka in around 125 BCE. At that time, the Buddhist Scriptures, known as the Theravadin Pali canon, were written on palm leaves. Over two hundred years later, when Kanishka called his Council in Kashmir, he commissioned around 500 monks to produce a commentary on the Buddhist scriptures, which became known as the *Mahavibhasia* ("Great Exegesis"). The significance of Kanishka's Council at Kashmir, is that it laid the foundation for Mahayana Buddhism which was a departure from the more orthodox Theravada tradition of the Sri Lankan Council. Not surprisingly, both Kanishka's Council and the *Mahavibhasia* exegesis, were rejected by the Theravadins, a situation that largely remains to this day.

King Kanishka was a great patron of Mahayana Buddhism and Gandhara became an important pilgrim centre as well as a transit point for monks taking the message of the Buddha from India to China. Gandhara was also the centre of Greco-Buddhist art, with workshops employing skilled craftsmen in the mass production of Buddhist sculptures. Gandhara was also a translation centre where hundreds of monks translated Buddhist texts from Pali into Chinese for onward transmission to China.

Unfortunately, many of these artefacts and manuscripts were looted or destroyed as a result of the Anglo-Afghan Wars (1839-1919), the Soviet-Afghan War (1979-1989) and the recent Afghan Civil Wars. What has survived, is kept in the British Library, the University of Washington and the Kabul Museum.

By around 225, the western part of the Kushan Empire had fallen to the rising Sassanids. The eastern territories were invaded from the North by the Huns and the Gupta Empire from the East. The Kushan Empire finally came to an end in 375.

The Sassanid Empire: 224-651 CE

The Sassanid Empire, also known as the Empire of the Iranians, or the Neo-Persian Empire is considered to be the peak of Iranian civilisation and was the last Persian power to exist before the arrival of Islam. It was named after Sassan, who was the grandfather of Ardashir I, the founder of the Empire. Ardashir was born in Fars, also known as Pars or Persis, which is the derivation of the name Persia.

Coming from Fars, the Sassanians viewed themselves as being truly Persian and therefore the rightful descendants of the ancient Persian Achaemenids. The Seleucids and Parthians, on the other hand, had been strongly influenced by the alien culture of Hellenism. Consequently, throughout their reign, the

Sassanids aimed to reduce Greek and Hellenistic influence in favour of Persian culture. Central to this policy was the promotion of Zoroastrianism, although throughout most of the Sassanian period, other religions, especially Judaism and Christianity, were tolerated.

Ardashir I: 224-242 CE

There are various sources, with differing accounts, as to how Ardashir, also known as 'the Unifier', came to power. The general consensus is that his, grandfather, Sassan, was warden of the Zoroastrian temple at Istakhr, three miles from the ancient city of Persepolis. Many of the stones used to build the temple had been taken from the ruins of Persepolis that was previously sacked by Alexander the Great. (See Chapter 3) For a short time, Istakhr was the capital city of the Sassanids and it remained an important centre for Zoroastrianism for many centuries and well into the Islamic period.

Papak, Ardashir's father, was both a grand priest of the temple and the king of Pars, which was a vassal state of Parthia. When Papak died in 222, Ardashir seized the throne of Pars from his brothers and assumed the title King Ardashir V of Pars. He then went on campaign conquering the western parts of Parthian territory. After several minor battles, Artabanus IV, the Parthian King of Kings, finally decided to confront him.

On 28th April, 224, a battle took place between Ardashir and Artabanus, possibly at Ramhormoz in the Khuzestan Province of today's Iran. Ardashir was accompanied by his son and successor, Shapur, together with around 10,000 Cavalry wearing Roman-style flexible chainmail. Although the Parthian troops were greater in number, they were at a disadvantage due to their heavier, leather armour, which was typical of the Parthian military. Artabanus, the last King of Kings of the Parthian Empire was killed in battle. So, ended the long line of Arsacid rulers, while Ardashir became the founder and first King of Kings of the House of Sassan. He was crowned *Shahanshah* at the ancient city of Ctestiphon, while his wife was crowned *Adhur-Anahid* (Queen of Queens). He established his capital city at Gur, today's Firuzabad, where remains of his palace can still be seen today.

Ardashir believed that he was destined to rule by divine right. He self-identified with the semi-mythical Kayanian dynasty, whose heroes feature in the *Avesta*, the sacred text of Zoroastrianism. In about 235, he commissioned work on a rock relief depicting his investiture. The location of the relief is at *Naqsh-e Rostam*, the necropolis of the Achaemenids, which was near Persepolis. The work, which can still be seen, shows *Ahura Mazda*, the highest deity of Zoroastrianism, handing Ardashir the ring of kingship. Both men are on horseback. Artabanus, the last Parthian king is shown being trampled beneath the hooves of Ardashir's horse, while the *Ahriman* (the devil) is trampled beneath the horse of *Ahura Mazda*. The inscription, written in Middle Persian, Parthian and Greek, reads: "*This is the figure of Mazdaworshiper, the lord Ardashir, Shahanshah of Iran, whose lineage is from Gods, the son of the lord Papak, the king*". Clearly Ardashir's motive for commissioning the work was to legitimise his overthrow of the Parthians and his subsequent rule of 'Iran', by divine right. The inscription bears the first known reference to 'Iran'. While initially the name 'Iran' appeared in a religious context, in time the word came to describe a geographical region.

After conquering Parthian territory in the West, Ardashir gained the submission of Turkmenistan, Chorasmia (modern Khwarezm) and Balk in Afghanistan. He then annexed Mosul in today's Iraq and also Bahrain in the Persian Gulf.

Shapur I: 240-270 CE

According to the sources, Ardashir named Shapur as his successor on the grounds that he was "*the gentlest, wisest, bravest and ablest of all his children*". (Shapur Shahbazi, 'SAPUR I:History *Encyclopaedia Iranica*), Certainly, Shapur had probably proven his military ability during the battle against Artabanus, when father and son fought side by side. Also, since accounts of the time refer to 'two kings', it is thought that Ardashir and Shapur shared the crown for approximately a year before Ardashir died.

Throughout the four hundred years of Sassanid rule, the Empire was constantly at war with Rome, as each power fought for control over the Eastern Mediterranean and Iranian plateau. There were two major campaigns during the reign of Shapur. The first came in 242-4, when the Sassanids captured the city of Hatra. During the battle, the young Roman Emperor Gordianus III was killed and Philip the Arab was proclaimed Emperor. Roman sources record that Philip made a shameful peace treaty with Shapur and ceded Armenia to the Sassanids, along with the payment of 500,000 dinars as ransom for his life.

The best-known of Shapur's campaigns was in around 260, when the Roman Emperor Valerian, and his senior troops, were captured at Edessa and sent as prisoners to Pars. Valerian spent the rest of his life in captivity and Shapur marked the event with another rock-face relief at *Naqsh-e-Rustam.* The capture of the Roman Emperor has also been portrayed in other art forms down the centuries, for example, Hans Holbein the Younger's 1571 sketch entitled 'The Humiliation of Valerian". At the time, many Christians believed Valerian's downfall to be punishment for his persecution of Christians under Roman rule.

As the Sassanids made inroads into Roman-held Mesopotamia and Syria, they acquired wealthy cities and valuable manpower. Those captives who had previously worked on Roman roads, viaducts and bridges, were particularly prized. Shapur and his successors employed them across the Sassanid empire in the construction of dams, bridges and new cities such as Bishapur, in today's Pars Province and Nishapur in northeast of Iran.

Religious Policy

Shapur I, like his father, promoted Zoroastrianism. He founded new fire altars and temples and raised the status of Zoroastrian priests, who accompanied troops on campaign. At the same time, he was tolerant towards other religions. Among the captives who were relocated from Syria to other parts of Shapur's Empire, were many Christians who discovered that life under the Sassanids offered a religious freedom unknown under the

Romans. Under Shapur, they were able to build their own churches, monasteries and establish bishoprics.

Shapur I also had a good relationship with the Jewish community. For example, Rabbi Samuel, who was head of the Yeshiva at Nehardea in Babylonia, encouraged the Jews to be loyal to the victorious Persians. It is said that Samuel was looking towards the Messianic Era and he possibly believed that Shapur I would be instrumental in restoring the 3rd Temple at Jerusalem, just as his predecessor, Cyrus the Great, had helped restore the 2nd Temple. (See Chapter Two)

Apart from the presence of Christians and Jews, Manicheans were growing in number. Named after their founder, Mani, Manicheans were influenced by Gnosticism. Gnostics believed in a dualistic cosmology whereby all things material, including the body, were bad and had been created by a lesser god, while the pure realm of the spirit, is the creation of the supreme, unknowable God.

The founder of the religion, Prophet Mani, was born in 216 in the Parthian vassal state of Seleucia-Ctesiphon. His father was a member of a Jewish/Christian sect of the Elcesaites, which was a branch of the Gnostic Ebionites. When Mani was just 12, and again at 14, he received visions from his 'spiritual twin', telling him that he should leave his home and travel to India. While in India, he learned about Hinduism, elements of which he then incorporated into his own Manicheaistic thought. The doctrine of reincarnation is one example and he came to believe that he was the reincarnation of Zoroaster, the Buddha and Jesus.

Mani wrote six major works in Syriac and another, the *Shabuhragan,* was written in Middle Persian and specifically dedicated to Shapur I. During the reign of Shapur I and the brief reign of his son, Hormizd I, Manicheanism flourished and Mani was a frequent visitor to the royal court. However, when Bahram II came to the throne in 274, everything changed. He was a staunch supporter of Zoroastrianism and under pressure from the priests he began a systematic persecution of Mani and his followers. In 274 Mani was imprisoned and died within a month.

Some accounts claim that he was flayed alive, and his skin stuffed with straw. The grim effigy was then hung over the main gate of the city of Gundeshapur as a warning to his followers, many of whom fled to India and China.

Generally speaking, Christians fared well under the Sassanids until Constantine the Great became Roman Emperor in 307. Under Constantine, two Edicts were passed: the Edict of Toleration (311), ending Diocletian's persecution of Christians, and the Edict of Milan (313), legalising Christianity across the Roman Empire. These Edicts changed the status of Christians, who became much more powerful throughout the Roman Empire. However, the Romans were long-term enemies of the Persians and the Sassanids feared that Christians in the Persian Empire might collaborate with Roman Christians, a situation that could threaten the security of the Sassanids. Consequently, Bahram II endeavoured to persuade his Christian elite to convert to Zoroastrianism. At the same time, all religious minorities faced increased discrimination.

Khosrau I: 531-579

One of the greatest of the Kings of Kings was Khosrau I, also known as the 'philosopher King' or 'ideal King'. He is best known for his major reforms as well as his patronage of the arts, sciences and philosophy, much of which was later inherited by Islam.

A significant change under Khosrau was the introduction of a new social class of small landowners (*deghans*). Previously, society was broadly divided into three groups: the priests, the nobility and the peasants. Functioning as a feudal society, the landowning nobility had ruled with considerable autonomy and held great power. They had maintained their own armies and raised their own taxes. Khosrau reformed the military system whereby the small landowners became the backbone of a new centralised army, rather than the previous system whereby the army was raised by feudal levy.

At the same time, Khosrau reformed the taxation system. Previously, the nobility had been exempt from paying taxes.

Under the new scheme, all landowners, large and small, were liable to taxation. Rates were set according to the amount and type of yield produced, e.g. date palms, olives, etc. Furthermore, all taxes were to be submitted directly to the central government rather than through 'middle-men', or tax-gatherers as previously. Another important element of Khosrau's centralisation policy was a reduction in the number of *satrapies* in favour of the establishment of four distinct provinces, with each province having its own garrison town and 'royal city'.

Decline of the Sassanids

In around 453, Yazdegerd II (435-457) was forced to move to the east in order to deal with invading Hephthalites, or White Huns, who had settled in Bactria. For the next hundred years or so, the Hephthalites and Sassanids were at times allies, at other times enemies. By 600, the Hephthalites were strong enough to invade Sassanid territory as far as Spahan (today's Isfahan Province). They finally submitted to the invading Arab Muslims in 705. (See Chapter Six)

Between 602 and 628, the Sassanids were at constant war with the Roman Byzantine Empire as each power fought for control over the Levant, Egypt, the Eastern Mediterranean and Asia Minor. In 614, Khosrau II (590-628) conquered Jerusalem and seized the True Cross, traditionally believed by Christians to be the remains of the cross on which Jesus was crucified.

With ongoing war in the East against the Hephthalites, and wars in the West with the Byzantines, the Sassanids were virtually bankrupt, both militarily and financially. The burden fell on the people, who were unable to pay higher taxes to pay for the wars, while at the same time livelihoods were lost due to social and economic breakdown.

The Byzantines took advantage of this situation and in 622, Heraclius, the Byzantine Emperor, launched a counter-offensive. Over the next five years, the two powers waged war, at huge human cost and the desecration of the most important fire temples. When peace was finally restored in 627, the Byzantines regained lost territory. But above all, they retrieved the True

Cross, which was taken ceremoniously back to Constantinople before finally returning it to Jerusalem.

Khosrau II was blamed for this humiliation in the face of the Byzantines and in 628, he was murdered on the orders of his son, Kavad II. During the following four years, chaos reigned and five different kings ruled. Civil war broke out and power fell to the Generals.

Yazdegerd III came to the throne in 632, at the age of eight. During his rule, Arabs, who followed the new religion of Islam, began to invade the Persian Empire. Yazdegerd spent most of his life trying to raise armies in order to repel the Arabs. When this failed he fled to Marw, in today's Turkmenistan, where he was apparently murdered by a miller. According to tradition, he was buried by Christian monks. His son and heir sought refuge in China.

Yazdegerd III was the last in a long line of the King of Kings. His death marked and end of the Sassanid Empire, which was the last Persian Empire before the arrival of Islam in Asia Minor, Central Asia and beyond.

Conclusion

The period between the fall of the Seleucids in 63 BCE and the arrival of Islam in the 7th Century, was a time of great change across Asia Minor and Central Asia. Along with the rise and fall of dynasties such as the Parthians, Kushans and Sassanids, the rising power of the Romans, first as Republic, then Empire and finally as the Eastern Roman Byzantines, changed the balance of power across the region. These changes in power inevitably happened within the context of war and desecration, resulting in the mass movement of people, either as refugees or captives. When people move, ideas move with them and consequently the period is also marked by cultural change.

One of the greatest changes was the gradual decline of Hellenism in favour of a restoration of Persian culture on the model of the Achaemenids. This did not happen suddenly, or uniformly. In the eastern provinces, for example, coins continued to be minted with Greek inscriptions, alongside images of Bactrian kings, well into the Parthian and Kushan periods. But probably the best examples of the survival of Hellenistic influence was in the form of Greco-Bactrian and Kushan art, often referred to as Gandhara art.

The survival and importance of Gandhara art is an example of the synthesis between Greek cultic religion and Buddhism. It was evidence of a widespread religious tolerance, the best example being under the Kushans who incorporated Hindu, as well as Greek, and Zoroastrian influences into their predominantly Buddhist culture. In terms of religion, the Kushans are probably best known for their patronage and transmission of Mahayana Buddhism from India to China.

In the western provinces, Jews and then Christians found refuge with the Persian Sassanids at a time when they were being persecuted by the Romans. This climate of religious tolerance continued until the conversion of Constantine the Great to Christianity and the consequent change in the status of Christians within the Roman Empire. From this point, the Persians feared that Christians living under Sassanid rule might collaborate with those of the Roman Empire. Thereafter, under pressure from the Zoroastrian priests, religious minorities suffered a degree of persecution.

The Parthians, Kushans and Sassanids were all located on the Silk Road and all benefited from the trade links between Rome and China. The Kushans in particular became a wealthy trading power equal to that of Rome and China. They developed trading posts along the Indus Valley that joined the east/west Silk Road, so expanding their network. This no doubt helped with their transmission of Buddhism to China.

The Parthians and their successors, the Sassanids had inherited territory in Western and Central Asia that was roughly equivalent to that of Alexander the Great. Consequently, they faced the same problem of trying to contain such a vast, multi-cultural, multi-ethnic empire. While the central region remained fairly stable, the periphery in the east and west was always vulnerable to attack. This meant that the Parthian and Sassanid rulers were constantly pulled from one end of their empire to the other in order to deal with the threat of rebellion and invasion.

From the 1st Century onwards, the Romans were the greatest threat in the West. Over the following few centuries the Roman Empire and the Persian Empires were at almost constant war. It was a situation that drained the resources of both powers. By the early 7th Century, the Sassanids were militarily and financially bankrupt as well as exhausted. They were too weak to resist the onslaught of a new wave of invaders from the deserts of Arabia, who were fired with the zeal of the new religion of Islam.

*****

CHAPTER SIX
The Arrival of Islam: 633-751 CE

When the Prophet Muhammed died in June 632, Abu Bakr became the first Caliph of the Rashidun (the 'Rightly Guided Ones', being the first four Caliphs following the death of the Prophet). Some of the Arab tribes thought that since Muhammed was dead, they were released from the commitment they had made to follow the new religion of Islam. This led to what is referred to as the 'Ridda Wars', or 'Wars of Apostacy'. In March 633, peace was restored and the entire Arabian Peninsula united under Abu Bakr. The following month, the first Arab Muslims invaded Sassanid and Byzantine territory.

This was not unusual. Small raiding parties had been happening for many decades. In order to protect themselves, the Byzantines and Sassanids allied with small independent Arab Kingdoms, so creating buffer states between themselves and the Arabian Peninsula. The Byzantines allied with Ghassanids and the Sassanids allied with the Lakhmids. Both states were Christian and were frequently at war with each other. Furthermore, at the time of the first Arab invasion in 633, relations between the two buffer states and their patrons, the Byzantines and Sasanids, were also at a low ebb. Consequently, the Ghassanids and Lakhmids welcomed an alliance with the Arab Muslims, who were culturally and linguistically closer to themselves.

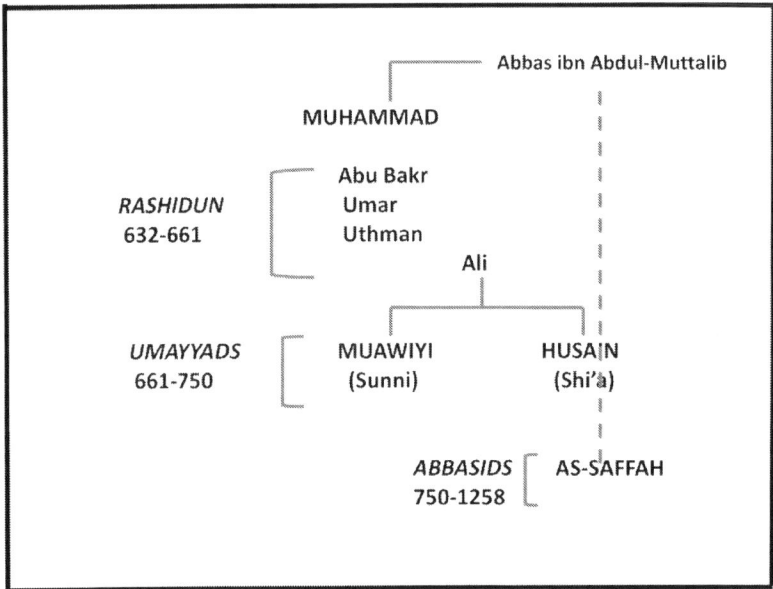

```
                                        ┌············· Abbas ibn Abdul-Muttalib
                                        │
                        MUHAMMAD        ┊
                                        ┊
                 ┌───    Abu Bakr       ┊
   RASHIDUN      │       Umar           ┊
   632-661       │       Uthman         ┊
                 │                 Ali  ┊
                 └───              │    ┊
                           ┌───────┴───────┐ ┊
   UMAYYADS      ┌    MUAWIYI         HUSAIN
   661-750       │    (Sunni)         (Shi'a)
                 └                        ┊
                                          ┊
                          ABBASIDS ┌  AS-SAFFAH
                          750-1258 └
```

First Arab Invasion: 633

In early 633, Al-Muthanna ibn Haritha led a raiding party into Mesopotamia. He seized a vast amount of loot and then retreated back into the Syrian Desert virtually unopposed. When he reported his success to the Caliph at Medina, Abu Bakr decided upon a full-scale invasion. The fact that under the peace treaty following the Ridda Wars, Muslim tribes were forbidden to raid each other, so being deprived of income, influenced his decision. An invasion into new territory, with the promise of a new source of loot, was politically expedient.

In preparation for the invasion, Abu Bakr placed General Khalid ibn Walid, a veteran of the Ridda Wars, in charge of a force of around 10,000 men. He was joined by tribal chiefs and their warriors. At this stage, all were volunteers and all were believers in the new religion of Islam. The objective of the invasion was to conquer the city of Hirah, close to today's Kufa, but Khalid first needed to gain the submission of the Ghassanids and Lakhmids. As an inducement, he offered both states freedom from the excessive taxation imposed by the Byzantines and Persians if they agreed to submit to Islam. Even if they did not convert, the *Jizya* tax, that was traditionally imposed upon non-Muslims, would be less oppressive than their current taxation.

Around the middle of March, 633, Khalid invaded Mesopotamia. Two months later, and having fought four battles, he succeeded in taking the city of Hirah. By the end of July, most of the territory of modern Iraq was under Muslim control. The following year, Damascus, which was then ruled by the Byzantines, also fell to the Muslims. Damascus later became the capital city of Umayyad Caliphate.

The Conquest of Mesopotamia:

With the Rashidun armies making inroads into Mesopotamia, the Byzantine Emperor Heraclius allied with the Sassanid Emperor Yazdegerd III, in an attempt to push the invaders back. To strengthen the alliance, Heraclius married his daughter to Yazdegerd. Some historians suggest that it was Heraclius's granddaughter who married Yazdegerd, which is quite possible considering that Yazdegerd was only about eleven, while Heraclius would have been in his sixties and probably had granddaughters of a marriageable age.

By this time, Umar ibn al-Khattab had succeeded Abu Bakr as Caliph of the Rashidun. In preparation for another invasion of Persia, this time, Umar recruited troops from across the Arabian Peninsula and he permitted ex-apostates to join the army. He also ordered that men from the same tribe or clan should fight alongside each other under their tribal flag, the purpose being that this should strengthen their loyalty to each other and help bind them into a united force. It is a tactic that has survived into modern times and comparable to the formation of regiments.

Two major battles took place in 636 that changed the course of history. The first was the Battle of Yarmouk between the 15th and 20th August. It was fought near the Yarmouk river, which separates Syria and Jordon, east of the Sea of Galilee. The result was a resounding victory for the Rashidun and the loss of Syria for the Byzantines.

The second was the Battle of Qadisiyyah, a small town near Kufa, in today's Iraq. In November 636, Umar appointed Sa'd ibn Abi Waqqas, another veteran of the Ridda Wars, as Commander. Soldiers from the earlier Battle of Yarmouk joined Sa'd's force, which eventually numbered some 36,000. In accordance with Islamic rules of engagement, Umar instructed Sa'd to first negotiate with the Sassanids, inviting them to convert to Islam. Should they agree, they would be left in peace. If they refused, then war was inevitable.

While the Persian leadership refused to convert, a large number of Persian and Byzantine elite troops did convert, and joined the Arab army. This was not sufficient to avoid war, however, and a four-day battle followed resulting in a resounding victory for the Muslims. The *Derafsh Kaviani*, or royal standard of the Sassanids, was captured, and after the jewels had been removed, it was sent to the Caliph in Medina, who ordered it to be burned.

The Battle of Qadisiyyah in 636, marked the beginning of the end of Sassanid rule in Iraq. Four months later, the imperial city of Ctesiphon fell. Islam now had a footing in Mesopotamia, which later provided a base for incursions deeper into Central Asia.

Arab Military

When the Arabs first invaded Persia, their military capability, with the exception of the archers was generally inferior to that of their enemies. Crucially, although they had an ample supply of camels, they had too few horses. But they could not be described as simple Bedouin raiders. On the contrary, they were well-organised, well-disciplined, well-trained and well-equipped.

The armour of the Rashidun military was modelled on that of the Byzantines and Sassanids. They wore helmets, often with the addition of a turban, that could be wrapped around the face as protection against the wind and sand. Their shields and Roman-style boots were usually made of leather.

The soldiers were provided with food, clothing and a salary. They were also granted land, or pensions, at the end of a campaign. But they were expected to provide their own weapons, which normally consisted of a bow and arrows, a spear up to 2.5 metres in length and a short straight sword. The weapons were made in Yemen from Indian woolz steel that had been imported by sea from southern India.

Initially, because of the lack of horses, the infantry outnumbered the cavalry. This changed as the Rashidun acquired both horses and weapons, such as the curved sword, as war booty. Later, the Arabs learned military skills and tactics from the peoples of Central Asia, some of whom had converted to Islam and joined the Rashidun cavalry, which by the end of the 7th Century, was using the stirrup.

Prisoners of war, particularly those from the Central Asian Turkic tribes, were often forced to join the Muslim armies as 'slave-soldiers'. They became known as Mamluks, which was the origin of the Mamluk Sultanate of Cairo (1250-1517).

Organisation

Under the Rashidun Caliphate, the army was divided into a regular standing army and a reserve force. The men were organised according to the decimal system, in units of tens, hundreds, thousands, etc. The army never marched on Fridays, being the Muslim holy day, and the route was determined by the availability of water. From the very beginning, espionage was an important element of warfare. Khalid ibn Walid, for example, relied heavily on Lakhmid spies in his conquest of Iraq.

Soon after taking Mesopotamia, Umar established garrison towns at Kufa and Basra. He appointed a Muslim General as Commander, together with a small number of Rashidun troops to keep order and maintain defence. Most of the local leadership, whose main responsibility was to collect local taxes, remained unchanged. This was a pattern that was to be repeated right across Central Asia.

Alongside the foundation of garrison towns, Umar instituted a registration system. While it initially only applied to the military, the system eventually came to incorporate all aspects of life under Rashidun rule. Known as the *Divan*, the registration system functioned as a government department with responsibility for all taxation, diplomatic relations, warfare and charitable affairs. Despite new innovations, the Rashidun maintained much of the earlier Persian infrastructure, including the communication and postal system, that had existed from the time of the Achaemenids.

Religion

Before the arrival of Islam, Christianity had been the predominant religion in Byzantine territory, and Zoroastrianism was the majority religion in the Persian Sassanid Empire. The earlier Sassanids had been tolerant towards adherents of other religions. However, this began to change under Khrusau I (531-579), when he put in process a series of reforms that raised the status of Zoroastrianism. Apart from commissioning the final canonisation of the sacred text, the *Avesta,* Khrusau ordered an increase in the number of sacred fires, temples and priests. This had the effect of bringing religion and state into a closer relationship, while at the same time increasing the divide between the ordinary people and the priestly class.

Before the Battle of Qadisiyyah, the Commander of the Rashidun Army invited the Persians to accept the message of the Prophet Muhammad and convert to Islam. Those Christians and Jews who refused to convert were placed under a status known as *dhimmi* whereby they had to pay a special tax *(Jizya)* in exchange for State protection and the freedom to worship. As *dhimmis,* however, they were treated as second-class citizens and denied access to certain positions. Those who converted to Islam were not only exempt from such taxation, but often received other financial incentives. In the eyes of the Arabs, however, they still remained second-class citizens.

Conversion was an attractive proposition to those Persians who had suffered the high taxation imposed by the Sassanids to pay for decades of warfare. Also, the simple theology of Islam and the egalitarian structure of the Islamic *Ummah* (community) offered a welcome alternative to Zoroastrianism, that was steeped in mysticism and ruled by an elitist priesthood.

Strictly speaking, Zoroastrians were not eligible for *dhimmi* status. According to Islamic law, only 'people of the book' i.e. those who could trace their descent from the Biblical Abraham, such as Jews, and Christians, could be granted *dhimmi* status. Despite this, Zoroastrians became *dhimmis* and in order to assist their understanding of Islam and encourage their conversion, they were permitted to read the Koran in their own language. Many of the early converts were either skilled workers or those engaged in industry. Because these workers often handled fire, which was a sacred element for Zoroastrians, they were seen as impure. Consequently, these 'impure ones' were frequently marginalised by society. In such circumstances, conversion to Islam proved to be an attractive proposition.

Conversion was relatively slow under the Rashidun (632-661) and the Umayyads (661-750). However, when the Abbasids came to power in the middle of the 8th Century, they embarked upon a more aggressive campaign of conversion. Zoroastrians began to suffer humiliation and persecution. Without the protection of the Sassanid state, their sacred buildings were desecrated, holy scriptures were burned and many priests were executed. By the 10th Century, Zoroastrians were outnumbered by Muslims, who had become the majority. Many of those Zoroastrians who refused to convert migrated to India, where they are known as Parsees.

The Conquest of Central Asia

The Battle of al-Qadsiyyah in 636, marked the completion of the conquest of Mesopotamia and for several years the Zagros Mountains became the boundary between the Rashidun and the retreating Sassanids. Over the next few years, the Sassanids sought alliances with the Chinese, the Parthians and other Bactrian tribes in an attempt to fight off the encroaching Arab forces. At this stage, the Chinese refused to help and the Parthians were already allying themselves with the Muslims. However, by 642 Yazdegerd believed that he had a large enough force to challenge the Rashidun. Despite the fact that his army was three times that of the Muslims, the Persians were defeated at the Battle of Nahavand, which is near today's Hamadan in

Iran. Yazdegerd III fled to Merv in Turkmenistan and the imperial army disintegrated into different factions under the leadership of warlords.

The Battle of Nahavand, known to Muslims as the 'Victory of Victories', marked a turning point in the Islamic conquest of Persia. From this point, the Rashidun began an all-out conquest of Central Asia. The Caliph controlled troop movements from Medina via messages to his commanders in the field. The commanders were usually commissioned for just one campaign, after which time they re-joined the ranks. This policy was aimed at maintaining equality in the army and avoiding the situation where one man became too powerful. It is markedly different to the practice in modern armies, where professional soldiers climb the ranks to that of General and above.

In 644, the Caliph in Medina was assassinated by a Persian captive, but his successor, Uthman ibn Affan, continued with the same military strategy as Umar.

Between 656 and 661, the Arab campaigns were interrupted because troops were needed to fight the First Fitna. This was the first civil war within the Muslim community. It was sparked by the assassination of Uthman ibn Affan, which led to conflicting views about the legitimacy of his successor, Ali ibn Abi Talib as fourth Caliph of the Rashidun, who was also the son-in-law of Prophet Muhammad. Eventually war broke out between the supporters of Ali, and the followers of Zubair ibn al-Awam Muawiyah I, who was opposed to Ali. In January 661, Ali was assassinated while praying at the Great Mosque in Kufa in Iraq. His son and successor, Hasan, made peace with Muawiyah. This marked the end of the Rashidun and the beginning of Umayyad rule with Muawiyah I as the first Caliph.

In October 680, some nineteen years later, another battle took place between the Umayyads and the family of Ali. The location was Karbala, in Iraq. It resulted in the death, or martyrdom, of Husain, who was the grandson of the Prophet Muhammad and brother of Hasan. Many of Husain's companions were also killed and most of his family were captured. The Battle of Karbala marked the schism between Sunni (followers of the way of Muhammad), who were the Umayyads and the Shi'a, who were the followers, or party, of Ali.

Abbasid Revolution: 750

The Rashidun and Umayyad periods were essentially a time when a feudal Arab minority ruled a non-Arab majority of Persians. During this time, an Arab military aristocracy lived in garrison towns and had little interaction with the local people. All non-Arabs, including those who had converted to Islam, were treated as second-class citizens. They were not permitted to enter the military or government service. Although converts to Islam were relieved of the *Jizya* tax, they were forced give up their Persian name in favour of an 'adopted' Arab tribal name.

As the Islamic conquest moved beyond Mesopotamia and into Central Asia, Arabs, including migrants from Arabia and particularly those from Yemen, began to live in areas outside the garrison towns. Consequently, they mixed with the people and there was even some inter-marriage, despite this being against Islamic law. With the majority of the population living as second-class citizens, under the rule of a minority Arab elite, rebellion was inevitable.

The first voices of discontent came from the region of Khorasan, which incorporated parts of today's north-east Iran, Central Asia and Afghanistan. Opposition to the Umayyads came from all sectors of society, but the Shi'a Muslims were the main protagonists. They whipped up a hatred towards the Umayyads by recalling the massacre of the Prophet's family at Kabala at the hands of the Umayyads. Furthermore, by way of propaganda, they declared that the Prophet's grandson, Husain, had married a Sassanid princess and he was therefore a legitimate successor through marriage in the long line of Persian royalty.

Another voice of discontent came from those Persians who had converted to Sunni Islam, but had always been treated as second-class citizens by the Arab 'super-tribe'. Zoroastrians, who had suffered religious discrimination under the Umayyads, also joined the rebels.

The rallying call for the rebellion was centred around the name of Abbas ibn Abd al-Muttalib, who was an uncle of the Prophet Muhammad. Taking his name, the revolutionaries became known as the Abbasids. In June 747, the first uprising took place in Merv, when around 10,000 soldiers under the command of Abbasid General Abu Muslim, marched under a black banner. The black banner became the flag of the Abbasids and in recent years has been adopted by the so-called Islamic State.

In January 750, the Abbasids finally defeated the Umayyads at the Battle of the Zab, on the banks of the Euphrates in Iraq. This marked the end of the Umayyad Caliphate and the beginning of the Abbasid Caliphate that was to last until 1258, when Baghdad fell to the Mongols, at which time the Abbasid Caliphate relocated to Cairo where it survived until 1517.

From the outset, the Abbasid Caliphate was multi-ethnic and inclusive. The people were registered for military and civil purposes according to location rather than tribe. The *dhimmi* system was abolished, along with the *jizya* tax and non-Muslims became known as *kafirs.*

Many of the Khorasians who had previously been guards under the Umayyad Caliphate now became generals in the Abbasid army and Persians became the officers and secretaries of the new State. At the same time a new institution, that of the Vizierate, was established with members of the Persian aristocracy assuming the role of Vizier. According to *Encyclopaedia Iranica,* there are two possible sources for the term 'vizier'. In Persian, the word 'wizir' meant decision, while in Arabic, the word 'vazir' takes its origin from reference to Aaron as the 'helper' (vazir) of Moses. Whatever the original source, the position of Vizier became extremely powerful. During Ottoman times for example, it was not unusual for the Vizier to be the true power behind the throne of a weak Sultan.

While the Arabs slowly lost influence, the Abbasids became more monarchical and resurrected much of the pomp and ceremony of the centuries-long traditions of the Persian court. The Abbasid period is also remembered as the 'Golden Age' of Islam. Some of the greatest poets, scientists, philosophers, historians and geographers came from the cities of Central Asia at the time of the Abbasid rule. For example, the famous polymath, Ibn Sina (980-1037), better known in the West as Avicenna, was born in Bukhara, today's Uzbekistan. And Omar Khayyam (1048-1131), the mathematician, astronomer and poet, was born in Nishapur, in the Khorasan Province of today's Iran.

According to tradition, a copy of Rashidun Caliph Uthman's original Koran is still kept in Tashkent. And Samarkand, also in today's Uzbekistan, became the first paper-making centre after China. The theory is that during the Abbasid/Chinese wars (see below), Chinese captives who were taken to Samarkand, passed on their skills of making paper out of rags, to the Muslims.

Transoxiana

Transoxiana was the region between the Rivers Amu Darya (Oxus) and Syr Darya (Jaxartes), and corresponds to today's Uzbekistan, Tajikistan and parts of Kyrgyzstan and Kazakhstan. Historically the area had been ruled at various times by the Greco-Bactrians, Yuezhi, Kushans and Hephthalites. Under the Seleucid and Sassanid Dynasties, much of the region was held under loose vassalage and at the time of the Islamic invasion, some tribes were vassals of the Chinese Tang Dynasty.

The people were broadly divided into Iranian-speaking tribes who lived in urban cities, some of which were along the Silk Road, and Turkic-speaking nomadic tribes. Medieval Muslim writers described the Turks as being similar to the Tibetans, with broad faces and small eyes. Crucially, all the tribes, or principalities, were fiercely independent. The forming of alliances was commonplace, but equally the tribes were prepared to change sides at will.

Transoxiana, with its wild mountain ranges, deep river gorges and remote oasis cities, proved to be the most difficult region for the Muslims to conquer. During the Umayyad period, invasions were limited to sporadic raids. However, the Arabs still posed a threat and so in 715, the Chinese sent 10,000 troops to Ferghana to defend the tribal states. When the Abbasids came to power in

750, the situation changed. Having defeated the Umayyads, they were now in a position to embark upon a serious campaign to take the rest of Central Asia.

The Abbasids secured an alliance with the Tibetan Empire, which at the time ruled large parts of East, Central and South Asia, against the Tang Chinese and their Turkic Karluk mercenaries. Between May and November, 751, a fierce battle took place in the valley of the River Talas, in today's Kazakhstan. The result was a victory for the Abbasids, partly because the Karluks defected to the Abbasids.

The Battle of Talas was the last battle in the Islamic conquest of Central Asia. The Abbasids made no attempt to take further territory in the East, and the Tang became preoccupied with the An Lushan rebellion, an internal uprising that threatened the survival of the Tang dynasty. Indeed, from this point, the Abbasids came to the aid of the Chinese in their efforts to put down the rebellion and many Muslims eventually settled in China, intermarried, and became the forerunners of some of China's current Muslim communities.

Conclusion

The real impetus for the invasion of Mesopotamia began following the Ridda Wars in 632-633. One outcome of these wars was an injunction upon the tribes of the Arabian Peninsula to stop raiding each other and to live in peace. Consequently, with the loss of booty from neighbouring tribes, the Arabs began small-scale raids into Mesopotamia. When these proved to be both militarily successful and resulted in the acquisition of considerable booty, the Caliph ordered a full-scale invasion.

Despite the fact that the Arab military at the time was inferior to that of the Byzantines and Persians, both those powers were exhausted, financially and militarily, from decades of warfare. This gave the Arab forces an advantage and by 634 Damascus in Syria had fallen, followed by al-Qadisiyyah in Iraq in 636. The Sassanid Empire finally collapsed at the Battle of Navahand in 642. Further conquest was interrupted in 656, by the outbreak of the First Fitna, the civil war that concluded with the founding of the Umayyad Dynasty.

Under the Umayyads, an Arab tribal elite ruled a majority of Persians. All non-Arabs, even those who converted to Islam, were treated as second-class citizens, a situation that eventually led to a revolution by a group claiming allegiance to Muhammad's uncle, Abbas ibn Abdul-Muttalib.

When the Abbasids came to power, the earlier restrictions imposed by the Umayyads were swept away. Persians moved into high military and government positions. Persian became the language of bureaucracy, while Arabic was the language of religion. Conversions to Islam increased while Zoroastrianism declined resulting in many Zoroastrians seeking refuge in India.

The wild and mountainous regions of Transoxiana proved to be much more difficult for the Abbasids to conquer. Apart from the resistance put up by fiercely independent tribes, the region was also contested by Tang China. The defeat of the Chinese at the Battle of Talas in 751 marked the end of Abbasid expansion eastwards and the beginning of relative friendly relations with China. This opened up trade opportunities and the exchange of people and ideas between the Abbasids and the Tang.

The Abbasid period is known as the 'Golden Age' of Islam. Its multi-ethnicity allowed for an exchange of ideas that enriched society. It was a period of great cultural flowering and scientific innovation.

The Islamic invasion of Central Asia marked a turning point in the history of the world. It resulted in a synthesis between Arab and Persian culture. Abbasid relations with China led to new ideas and skills spreading westwards and eventually into Europe. Finally, the invasion marked a shift in Islam's powerbase from its Arab heartland into Asia, and its transformation from a tribal, into an international, religion.

*****

CHAPTER SEVEN

The Great Seljuk Empire: 1037-1194

The Iranian Intermezzo

The period between the decline of Abbasid rule in the middle of the 10th Century and the rise of the Seljuk Turks in the middle of the 11th Century, is known as the Iranian Intermezzo. During this time, while the Abbasids remained the titular rulers, various Iranian and Turkic dynasties vied for power across the region. The most significant of these were the Buyid Dynasty (934-1062) and the Ghaznavid Dynasty (977-1186).

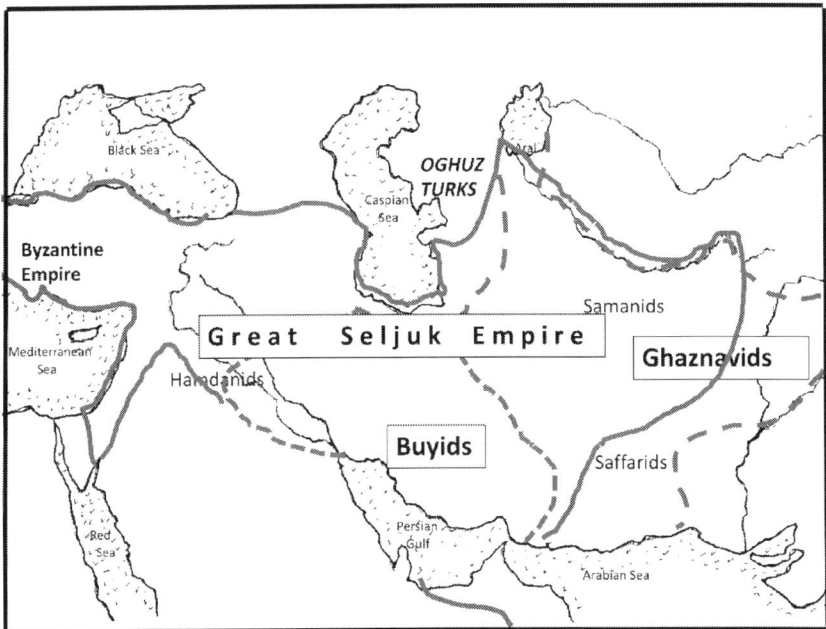

The Buyids were Shi'a Muslim Iranians who came from the mountainous Daylamite region that bordered the southern coast of the Caspian Sea. They had fought as mercenaries under the Sassanids and were known for their skills in shield formation. Throughout their 130-year rule, the Buyids remained fiercely anti-Arab and promoted Iranian culture and traditions. For example, 'Adud al-Dawla, who ruled from 949-983, used the ancient Persian title of King of Kings, (Shahanshah).

As the Buyids gradually extended their territory, they found it necessary to recruit Turks and Kurds into their army. This led to tensions between the Daylamite Buyids, who were Shi'a, and the Turks and Kurds, who were Sunni Muslims. Consequently, the Buyids frequently appointed Nestorian Christians to senior positions in the military and government as a way of preserving stability.

At its height, the Buyid Dynasty ruled an area incorporating most of today's Turkey, Iran, Iraq, Kuwait and Syria as well as parts of Oman and the UAE. Before its fall to the Seljuks in 1062, the Buyid Dynasty was the most powerful in the region.

While the Buyids dominated western Central Asia, the Turkic Ghaznavids rose to power in the east. Since the Ghaznavids were originally slave guards of the Sassanids, they were known as Mamluks and from their base in Ghazni, in today's Afghanistan, they repeatedly invaded India. In the process, the religion of Islam, which first arrived with Muslim traders in the 7th Century, spread deeper into the Indian peninsula. As a consequence, although Afghans held the most senior positions in the Ghaznavid military, Hindus were increasingly recruited into the ranks and the use of war elephants became commonplace.

The Ghaznavids acquired immense wealth from the plunder of Indian palaces, which they then used to build their own mosques and cities. Their capital city of Ghazni became the cultural centre of the eastern Islamic world. Although many of the city's great buildings subsequently fell into disrepair, its strategic importance, being close to Kabul, remains to this day and as recent as 2018, the Taliban fought for control over the city.

In 1040, the Ghaznavids lost the region of Khorasan to the Seljuk Turks at the Battle of Dandanaqan, which is near today's Merv. From this point on, the Seljuks made further inroads into the western part of Ghaznavid territory, until the dynasty finally fell to the Iranian Ghurid dynasty in 1186.

The Seljuks were a Turkic clan of the Oghuz Yabgu State. Coming from the region between the Caspian and Aral Seas, the dynasty lasted from about 750 to 1055. The founder of the dynasty was

Seljuk Beig, a warlord of the Oghuz Kinik tribe. In 985, the tribe split from the Oghuz confederacy and settled on the banks of the Jaxartes (Syr Darya). At this point, Seljuk Beig converted to Islam. Under Seljuk's grandsons, Tugrul and Chaghri Beg, the Seljuks migrated to Khurasan, where they defeated the Ghaznavids at the Battle of Dandanaqan in 1040.

Other Turkic dynasties that migrated westwards after the 11th Century and can trace their ancestry back to the Oghuzs, include the Ottomans, Safavids and Qajars.

Alp Arslan: 1063-1072

Muhammad bin Dawud Chaghri, great-grandson of Seljuk Beig, succeeded his uncle Tugrul as ruler of the Seljuks. Better known as Alp Arslan, meaning 'heroic lion', he was made Sultan of the Great Seljuk in 1064 and under his rule the Empire extended from the Oxus in the East to the Tigris in the West.

Prior to becoming Sultan, Alp Arslan had fought alongside Tugrul against the Shi'a Fatimids who were seeking to extend their territory from Egypt northwards into the Levant as far as Syria. When Alp Arslan succeeded Tugrul, he continued the fight against the Fatimids. However, in 1064, as his forces marched through Anatolia towards Syria, they invaded Byzantine territory, seizing Armenia and Georgia. Although a peace treaty was signed between the Byzantines and the Seljuks in 1069, sporadic fighting continued in the region of Cilicia between the two powers.

On the 26th August 1071, a decisive battle took place at Manzikert, north of Lake Van in the Mus Province of today's Turkey. At the time, the Byzantines were fighting on two fronts. They were defending their territory in southern Italy against the Normans, as well as fighting off the Seljuks in Anatolia. Consequently, they were forced to rely on Pecheneg and Cuman mercenaries, as well as Norman and Frank troops, to strengthen their military. The Byzantine army, which numbered around 20,000, was led by Emperor Romanos IV Diogenes. The Seljuk force, which included soldiers from Aleppo, was slightly greater in number and was led by Alp Arslan.

Initially the Seljuks were on the defensive. But then the Pecheneg and Cuman mercenaries changed sides and the Franks and Normans deserted the battle-field, leaving the Byzantines vulnerable. The result was a resounding victory for the Seljuks. The Byzantine Emperor was captured and escorted into the presence of Alp Arslan. He was forced to perform the ritual act of humiliation by kissing the ground before the feet of the Sultan. A famous conversation is then said to have taken place.

When Alp Arslan asked Romanos "What would you do, if I were brought before you as prisoner?", Romanos replied "Perhaps I would kill you, or exhibit you in the streets of Constantinople". Alp Arslan replied, "My punishment is far heavier. I forgive you and set you free". Romanos then remained a captive of Alp Arslan for a week, during which time they ate together while discussing peace terms. After Romanos agreed to the surrender of Antioch, Edessa, Hierapolis and Manzikert to the Seljuks, he was given many presents as well as an escort to see him back to Constantinople. The Sultan then turned eastwards with the intention of conquering Transoxiana. But he was captured along the way and on the 25th November, 1072, assassinated by the governor of a small fortress. His body was finally taken to Merv where he was buried alongside his father, Chaghri Beig.

The Battle of Manzikert marked a major turning point in the history of Europe and Asia Minor. It was the beginning of the slow decline of the Byzantine, or Eastern Roman Empire. It was the start of the Turkification of Anatolia, as well as the beginning of the Seljuk presence in the Levant. Crucially, the defeat of the Byzantines at the Battle of Manzikert alerted the Christian West to the threat of Islam and contributed to the call for the First Crusade.

Nizam al-Mulk, Vizier of the Seljuk Empire: 1064-1092

Alp Arslan was succeeded in 1072 by his son Malik-Shah I (Malik meaning 'King' in Arabic and Shah meaning 'King' in Persian). However, the real power lay in the hands of Abu Ali Hasan ibn Ali Tusi, better known as Nizam al-Mulk ('Order of the Realm'), who had been appointed Vizier of the Seljuk Empire by Alp

Arslan. Nizam al-Mulk had also been instrumental in paving the way for the accession of Malik-Shah by removing other contestants for the throne.

Nizam al-Mulk, who was Persian, was born in 1018 in Tus, today's Razavi in the Khorasan Province of Iran. His family were minor landowners and his father had worked for the Ghaznavids. Nizam became a scholar and in 1059, he was appointed Chief Administrator of Khorasan. As Vizier to Sultan Alp Aslan and particularly under Sultan Malik Shah I, he rose to become the *de facto* ruler of the Empire. While Malik-Shah commanded all military affairs, Nizam al-Mulk was responsible for administering the Empire and is known as the archetypal 'good vizier' of Islamic history.

One of Nizam's early tasks was to establish military fiefs that were governed by Turkic princes, or 'atabegs', who were often related to the Sultan. A key aim of the fiefs was to provide a means of integrating the nomadic Turkic tribes into settled Anatolian agricultural communities. These fiefs then provided both a military resource and also a financial resource through taxation, which meant that the Seljuks could become self-sufficient rather than depend upon vassal states.

Nizam al-Mulk is perhaps best known for his contribution to higher education and government policy. In terms of education, he founded numerous schools, or madrassahs. Thought to be the forerunner of today's madrassahs, they were named 'Nizamiyyah', after him. The schools, which were funded by the monarchy and aristocracy, provided a first-class higher education that was renowned throughout the Islamic world and across Europe.

The best-known of these schools was the Al-Nizamiyya university of Baghdad which was founded in 1065. In 1091, Nizam al-Mulk appointed the famous philosopher/theologian al-Ghazali as Professor. Tuition, which was free, was originally offered in Islamic studies, literature and arithmetic, but later included history, mathematics, science and music. Ibn Tumart, founder of the Almohad Dynasty of North Africa, was said to be a student under al-Ghazali, and the Persian poet Sa'di also studied at Al-Nizamiyya between 1195 and 1226. In 1258, Sa'di personally witnessed the destruction of the university by the Mongols. (See Chapter Eight)

Nizam al-Mulk's other great achievement was his treatise on good government. Known as the Siyasatnama, or Siya al-Muluk (Book of Government), it defined good governance based on historical precedence (including pre-Islamic history), and Islamic Law. The book comprised fifty chapters concerning religion and politics, as well as detailed guidance on the role of soldiers, spies and the police. The latter part of the Siyasatnama concerned the dangers threatening the Empire, and particularly the rise of the Ismailis. The work also stressed the need to protect the weak and emphasised that the ruler should live a life of piety, always mindful of his responsibility before God for his actions.

Nizam al-Mulk proved to be an able stateman. For example, he realised it was politically expedient to strengthen relations with the Abbasid Caliphate at Baghdad, which at the time held nominal power over the Seljuks. And he also managed to keep at bay the ongoing threat from the Shi'a Fatimids of Egypt. While Nizam's government was based on Sunni principals, these were not rigidly enforced and largely for pragmatic reasons, Shi'a and Sufi Muslims, as well as other minorities, were accommodated. An exception to this was his attitude towards the Shi'a Nizaris.

Towards the end of his life, Nizam lived under the constant threat of assassination, possibly on the order of Sultan Malik-Shah I. Indeed, with this in mind, it is said he frequently uttered the words "The crown falls with the removal of the ink-stand." As it happened, he was assassinated on the 14th October 1092, most likely by a member of the Nizari Ismaili State.

Nizari Ismaili State

The greatest internal threat facing the Seljuks during the reign of Malik-Shah I and his vizier Nizam al-Mulk, was from the increasingly powerful Shi'a Ismailis. The Ismailis take their name from Ismail ibn Jafar, who was the son of Ja'far al-Sadiq, the sixth

Imam according to mainstream Twelver Shi'a tradition. Following a succession crisis in around 750, the followers of Ismail split from the Twelvers (followers of twelve Imams), and became known as the Ismailis. The Fatimids of Egypt were Shi'a Ismaili and this is one of the reasons why the Fatimid Empire presented such a threat to the Sunni Seljuks.

In the 11th Century, another succession crisis occurred within the Fatimid Caliphate when Nizar al-Mustafa, the rightful successor to the Fatimid Imamate, was deposed. Nizar went on to found the Nizari branch of Shi'a Ismailism and his son, Ali al-Hadi ibn Nizar, escaped to Alamut in Persia where he found refuge among other Nizari followers and through him the Nizari Imamate continued. The majority of today's Ismailis, including the Agha Khan, who is the current Imam, belong to the Nizari branch of Shi'a Islam.

The majority of Ismailis in the 11th Century were to be found in Fatimid Egypt. However, there were also minority Ismaili communities living in Persia, Syria and Iraq. This was partly the result of Fatimid missionaries being sent out from Egypt to evangelise the people of the Levant and Mesopotamia. One such missionary was Hassan-i-Sabbah who was born in Qom, Iran, in around 1050 into a Twelver Shi'a family. When he was about 17 years, Sabbah converted to Ismailism and spent around three years in Egypt studying, before returning to Persia as a missionary. He then joined the Nizari sect, acknowledging Ali al-Hadi ibn Nizar as the rightful Imam.

At the time, the Shi'a of Persia and Syria resented the heavy taxation and degree of oppression imposed upon them by the Sunni Seljuk government. Consequently, they tended to live in remote communities beyond the reach of the authorities. Hassan-i-Sabbah supported the Nizaris and he soon came to the attention of Vizier Nizam al-Mulk, who called for his arrest on the grounds that he was an agitator.

In order to escape arrest and continue with his missionary work, Sabbah needed a safe hideout. His choice was a remote fortress called Alamut Castle which is located south of the Caspian Sea in today's Iranian province of Qazvin. The castle had been built at the end of the 9th Century, was virtually impregnable and in its two hundred years of existence, had never been conquered.

His first task was to convert the Shi'a Ismailis living in the surrounding villages to Nizarism, during which time he disguised himself as a schoolteacher. He then sent infiltrators into the castle in preparation for its eventual takeover. In 1090, Hassan-i-Sabbah seized the castle through a bloodless coup and paid the ruling Lord 3,000 gold dinars as compensation for his loss. This marked the foundation of the Nizari Ismaili State, also known as the Alamut State. The Nizaris eventually minted their own coins and controlled a network of castles across Syria and Persia.

The 'Order of the Assassins'

With the foundation of the Nizari Ismaili State, Sabbah founded the Order of the Assassins, with himself as Grand Master. Early information about the Assassins comes from either Sunni sources, which were derogatory, or the writings of Western Crusaders and European travellers. Marco Polo, for example, who is reputed to have stayed at Alamut castle, described Sabbah as 'the Old Man of the Mountain' and related how he drugged his young followers with hashish before sending them out to commit targeted political murders. In European sources, the link between the word hashish-takers and assassins became commonplace for several centuries. Although this theory is now generally disputed, the word 'assassin', meaning a politically motivated murder, has survived.

Unfortunately, most of the original records of the Order of the Assassins were destroyed by the Mongols when they attacked Alamut castle in 1256. More recently, however, Muslim writers have revisited the issue. For example, the Lebanese writer, Amin Maalouf claims that Sabbah usually called his followers *Asasiyun,* meaning 'people who are faithful to the foundation of the Faith'. (*Samarkand,* 1998, Interlink Publishing Group).

It is generally accepted that from an early age, Hassan-i-Sabbah was a keen student and studied many subjects including mathematics, philosophy, geography and metaphysics. During his time in Egypt he studied Ismaili theology as well as Sunni texts. Once he settled at Alamut he established a vast library and centre for learning. Unique to the Nizari sect, he insisted that Persian be the language for all holy literature and he had Nizari Persian texts distributed across Central Asia and Mesopotamia.

Hassan-i-Sabbah is best-known for his recruitment and training of young assassins. As a persecuted minority, the Nizaris were unable to form an army and therefore had no hope of challenging the Seljuks by the normal military means. Their alternative weapon was psychological warfare and the assassination of key figures in the enemy establishment. The first person to be assassinated was Nizam al-Mulk, vizier to the Seljuk Sultan Malik-Shah I.

The assassins were young and were the lowest among several ranks within Alamut Castle. They were recruited from the surrounding villages, indoctrinated into Nizari theology and because they might be sent to locations across the eastern Mediterranean, were schooled in foreign languages and cultures. Crucially, they eventually became completely devoted and obedient to the Grand Master.

The young men were known as *feda'i,* meaning one who would self-sacrifice for the sake of a particular cause. The targeted murders were usually carried out in public, in order to instil fear in the people. Consequently, the assassins had little chance of escape and expected to be captured, tortured and executed. In other words, they were prepared for suicide.

Hassan-i Sabbah died at Alamut Castle in 1124. He was succeeded by a further six Grand Masters before the fall of the Assassins to the Mongols in around 1275. The few who survived the Mongol invasion sought refuge in India. The Assassin castles situated in Syria submitted to the Mamluk Sultanate, which had overthrown the Ayyubid Dynasty of Cairo in 1250.

Between 1090, when the Nizari Ismaili State was founded, and their fall in 1250, victims of assassination included two Caliphs, and several viziers and Sultans. Although the Seljuks were the initial enemy of the Assassins, over time they carried out political assassinations on behalf of other powers, for example, the Fatimids and even the Crusaders. The first Crusader to be murdered was Count Raymond II of Tripoli in around 1130. Their most celebrated Frankish victim was the Marquis Conrad of Montferrat, King of Jerusalem, who was assassinated in 1192, rumoured to be on the order of Richard, King of England. Several unsuccessful attempts were also made on the life of Salah ad-Din, better known in the West as Saladin.

The life of Hassan-i Sabbah, and the Order of the Assassins, has since spawned an industry in books, films and video games. For example, the video game, 'Assassin's Creed, published in 2007 by Ubisoft, has sold around 73 million copies worldwide.

The Crusades:

Sultan Malik-Shah I died on the 19th November 1092, thought to be from poisoning, possibly on the order of the Abbasid Caliph. Interestingly, the timing of his death fits with Nizam al-Mulk's prediction that the 'crown will fall with the removal of the inkstand'; Nizam being the 'inkstand', who had been assassinated the previous month by the Assassins.

When Malik-Shah I died, there followed a succession crisis. Consequently, the Empire was divided between his brother and his sons. His son Mahmud I inherited Persia and his brother Tutush gained Syria. When Tutush died in 1094, Syria was further divided among his own sons into even smaller states, or emirates. Other significant successor states included the Sultanate of Rum under Kilij Arslan ('Sword Lion') in western Anatolia, and the Danishmends, founded by Danishmend Gazi, in eastern Anatolia. Such fragmentation led to on-going intrigue and constant infighting between the various rulers, or emirs. This was the situation in Anatolia on the eve of the First Crusade.

The origins of the First Crusade, also known as the Princes' Crusade, can be traced back to the Battle of Manzikert in 1071, when the Seljuk Sultan Alp Arslan defeated the Byzantines and captured Emperor Romanos IV. This event caused alarm among the Christian Byzantines, who feared that the Seljuks would reach Constantinople. Over the next twenty years, the Byzantines fought hard to defend their territory against the advancing Seljuks.

In March 1095, the Byzantine emperor Alexius I Comnenus sent ambassadors to the Council of Piacenza in Italy to ask the Pope for mercenaries to join their forces against the Seljuks. Although previous such requests had been rejected, this time Pope Urban II responded positively. Relations between the Papacy in Rome, and the Patriarchy in Constantinople, had been strained ever since the schism resulting in a split between the Western Latin Church and the Eastern Orthodox Church in 1054. It has been speculated that Pope Urban's willingness to help the Byzantines in 1095 might have been motivated by his desire to reunite the Church, with himself as Head. It is equally likely that he saw this as an opportunity to unite the often-warring western aristocracy against a common enemy. Either way, his call to arms was as much, if not more, a question of political expediency as it was about religious duty.

Pope Urban II launched his call to arms in November 1095 at the Council of Clermont, then in the Duchy of Aquitaine. Several versions of the Pope's speech were recorded, but that written by the chronicler Fulcher of Chartres is considered one of the most reliable. Fulcher was a priest and was most likely present at the Council. He joined the Duke of Normandy on the First Crusade and became chaplain to Baldwin of Boulogne when the latter became King of Jerusalem.

According to Fulcher, the Pope called on 'those who had been robbers, to now become knights, those who had been fighting each other, to now fight the barbarians and those who had fought as mercenaries for a pittance, to now fight for eternal life'. Another version of the speech, written by Robert the Monk, was far more dramatic. He described the atrocities of the infidels, claiming that they desecrated churches, committed forced circumcision, carried out beheadings, torture, disembowelling and rape. Both chroniclers record how the Pope promised the remission of sins for all who died on the journey to the Holy Land, or in battle against the pagan.

Historians have long debated the extent to which the First Crusade was aimed at helping the Byzantines defend their territory, or to liberate Jerusalem. None of the various versions of the Pope's speech at Clermont are very specific, apart from the need to defend Christians and their Churches. Furthermore, from the time Jerusalem first fell to the Rashidun Caliphate in 638 CE, Christians had continued to live in Jerusalem and pilgrims had travelled to the holy city relatively unharmed, apart from the normal threat of bandits etc. Although Christians inevitably suffered from the consequences of the ongoing conflict between the Fatimids and Seljuks over the possession of Jerusalem, they were more likely to have been casualties of war, than victims of persecution. With this in mind, Robert the Monk's description of Seljuk atrocities committed against Christians, is most likely exaggerated.

Between the spring and autumn of 1096, an estimated 60,000 men, women and even children left Europe for the Holy Land. The first group, known as the People's Crusade, led by Peter the Hermit, was little more than an undisciplined rabble. As they travelled across Europe and along the Rhine they pillaged villages and murdered hundreds of Jews. The atrocities committed against Jews by Crusaders became known as the Rhineland Massacres.

The People's Crusade got as far as Nicaea, which was previously under the Byzantines, but by 1096 it was the capital of the Seljuk Sultanate of Rum. Here they were soundly defeated by the 17-year-old Sultan Kilij Arslan's more experienced troops. While Peter the Hermit escaped, the majority of his followers were massacred. Having defeated the People's Crusade, Kilij turned his attention to his other enemy, the Turkish Danishmends.

In August 1096, four separate armies left Europe, each taking a different route and each led by a prince or duke, hence the combined force was known as the Princes' Crusade. This time the troops were more disciplined and better trained. The armies converged at Constantinople. Despite the fact that their leaders were Normans, and therefore enemies of the Byzantines, they were well received by the Emperor who offered hospitality, and some of his own troops, for the onward journey.

Crusader States (*Outremer)*

The Byzantine Emperor and leaders of the Crusade agreed between them that should a city that had previously been part of the Byzantine Empire be liberated, then it should be returned to the Byzantines. In June 1097, when Nicaea was liberated, the Crusaders reluctantly handed it back. This was not the case with Antioch, which was taken in June 1098.

In October, 1097, Prince Bohemund of Taranto, who was the Norman ruler of Taranto in Southern Italy, laid siege to the city of Antioch. The city was heavily fortified, having 12,000 metres of walls and 350 turrets. But with the help of a Christian Armenian guard, the Crusaders gained entry.

A few days later, a Muslim army from Mosul, commanded by the governor and warlord Kerbogha, arrived to relieve the city. Consequently, the Crusaders now found themselves trapped within the city walls. As winter approached, the crusaders began to run out of food and water. They were forced to eat horse-flesh and, some say, even human-flesh. The siege came to an end in June 1098, when, according to tradition, the Crusaders discovered the holy lance that had pierced Christ's side, under the foundations of the Cathedral of St. Peter. With renewed spiritual strength, Bohemund's troops then marched out of the city and miraculously defeated the besieging Muslims.

Prince Bohemund of Taranto then claimed the title Prince of Antioch and established the Crusader State of the Principality of Antioch. This was contrary to the agreement made with the Byzantine Emperor and it further alienated the Byzantines at a time when the relationship between the Western Church in Rome and Eastern Church in Constantinople was already fragile.

Three other Crusader States were founded by the Crusaders in the Levant; the County of Edessa, the County of Tripoli and the Kingdom of Jerusalem. The citizens of Edessa, as with Antioch, were predominantly Armenian and Greek Orthodox Christians.

In the case of Edessa, Baldwin of Boulogne became Count of Edessa after negotiating a peaceful surrender with its ruler, Thoros. He then married Thoros's daughter, Arda of Armenia, who later became Queen of Jerusalem when Baldwin became King.

The founding of the Kingdom of Jerusalem in July 1099, was far from peaceful. After a three-year journey, during which time many died, some stopping along the way, and others turning back, the remnant arrived at the walls of Jerusalem. A month-long siege followed. When the Crusaders finally breached the walls, a whole-sale massacre took place. Muslims, and many Christians who were often indistinguishable from the Muslims, were slaughtered and hundreds of Jews were burned alive in a synagogue where they had taken refuge.

In 1102, Count Raymond of Toulouse founded the County of Tripoli, which for a time became a vassal state of Jerusalem. It was the last Crusader State to be founded and it was to be the last to fall.

The Muslim Perspective

The Seljuks had been totally unprepared for what they saw as an invasion of their lands. The first knowledge they had of any potential threat came from Turkish mercenaries who were fighting for the Byzantines. They heard that hundreds of 'Franj' (the Muslim term for 'Frank') were approaching Constantinople, and that they were pillaging villages and generally causing havoc.

When the Princes' Crusade invaded a few months later, Kilij Arslan was caught totally off-guard. But the greatest problem for the Muslims at the time was that they could no longer present a united force in order to defend their territory. As mentioned above, when Malik-Shah I died in 1092, the Seljuk Empire fragmented into numerous independent states that spent most of their time fighting each other.

Things began to change in 1127 when Imad ad-Din Zengi, founder of the Zengid dynasty, assumed power in Mosul. In

1128, he succeeded in bringing Aleppo under his rule, followed by Damascus in 1130. In 1144, having reunited Syria, he managed to oust the Crusaders from Edessa, the most vulnerable of the Crusader States. The fall of Edessa led to the launch of the Second Crusade in 1147 which was aimed at regaining the city.

The Muslims were further strengthened with the rise of An-Nasir Salah ad-Din Yusuf ibn Ayyub, better known in the West as Saladin, who was an ethnic Kurd, born in 1137 in Tikrit, today's Iraq. In 1164, Saladin accompanied his uncle Shirkuh, who was a general in the Zengid army, to Egypt. Despite being a Sunni Muslim, Saladin won the trust of the Ismaili Fatimid ruler and was appointed Vizier. By 1174, Saladin had become Sultan of Egypt and Syria, as well as founder of the Ayyubid Dynasty. From his position of strength, Saladin was able to defeat the Crusaders at the Battle of Hattin on the plains of Galilee, in July 1187. He then went on to conquer the Crusader Kingdom of Jerusalem in October 1187.

Unlike the fall of Jerusalem to the Crusaders in 1099, which was a blood-bath, the surrender to Saladin in 1187 was relatively peaceful. Native Christians were permitted to stay in the city, while Crusaders and their families were allowed to leave, albeit on payment of a ransom. The majority of the Crusaders travelled to the Crusader city of Akko (Acre), on the northern coast of today's Israel. This was to be the last Crusader stronghold in the Levant, before it fell to the Mamluks in 1271.

While the independent Seljuk states in Anatolia and Syria were fighting off the Crusaders, they were unable to send troops to defend Seljuk states in Transoxiana. Consequently, the region suffered rebellion and also invasion from the Qara-Khitai, a nomadic Chinese dynasty, also known as the Western Liao Empire. By the beginning of the 13th Century, all that remained of the Great Seljuk Empire was the small Sultanate of Rum in Anatolia. But in 1243, the Sultanate of Rum fell to the Mongols.

Conclusion

Originating from the Qiniq branch of the Oghuz tribal Turkic federation, the Seljuks were the first ethnic Turks to rule over vast swathes of Central Asia and Anatolia. They would later be followed by other Oghuz tribes, including the Ottomans, the Safavids and the Qajars.

By the beginning of the 11th Century, although the Abbasid Caliphate in Damascus was still recognised as the nominal power across most of the Muslim world, vast areas of Central Asia were ruled by semi-independent Islamic states. During the same period, the Shi'a Fatimids of Cairo were becoming a growing threat as they challenged the Abbasids for control of the Levant.

As staunch Sunni Muslims, the Seljuks were naturally opposed to the Fatimids. In August, 1071, while marching towards the Levant with the aim of challenging the Fatimids, the Seljuk Sultan Alp Arslan came into conflict with the Byzantines at the Battle of Manzikert, capturing Emperor Romanos IV in the process. The fact that the Byzantines were then fighting the Normans in Italy, possibly contributed to their defeat due to depleted forces.

The Battle of Manzikert proved to be a watershed in the history of Europe and the Near East. It marked the beginning of a change in relations between Christians and Muslims. Although the Umayyads had conquered Jerusalem in the 7th Century, Christians had continued to live in the city and pilgrims travelled through Muslim-controlled territory in relative safety. However, the preaching of the First Crusade was couched in vitriolic terms that were aimed at portraying Muslims in a negative light. This 'demonising' of Islam continues to have repercussions to this day.

The events of the Crusades also affected relations between the Eastern Orthodox Church and the Western Catholic Church. While doctrinal and political tensions already existed, these were exacerbated by the unruly behaviour of the Crusader armies, the failure to hand back Antioch as previously agreed, and finally the sack of Constantinople in 1204 during the Fourth Crusade.

In theory, the Seljuk policy was one of tolerance towards minorities. One exception, however, was their attitude towards the Order of the Assassins that had been founded by the Nizari Ismaili State. As Shi'a Muslims, the Nazaris were often persecuted by the Sunni Seljuks. It is in this context that Hassan-i-Sabbah, Grand Master of the Order of the Assassins, established his remote headquarters at Alamut Castle from where he recruited and trained young assassins to carry out targeted political murders.

The Empire was probably at its height during the reign of Sultan Malik-Shah I, who commanded the military. He also succeeded in maintaining the balance of power between the Seljuks and the Abbasids and also keeping the Fatimids at bay. His Vizier, Nizam al-Mulk, was responsible for organising the Empire. He introduced major educational and governmental reforms and is known in the Islamic world as a 'model' vizier.

Under the Seljuks, Turkification spread into Anatolia and Syria, while the Seljuks adopted the Persian language and many elements of Persian culture. The result was a vibrant Persian-Turkic culture that found expression in architecture, scholarship and literature.

With the death of Malik-Shah I and the subsequent succession crisis, the Empire fell into decline and fragmentation. From this weakened position, the Seljuks had to face not only the Frankish invasion, known in the West as the Crusades, but also rebellion and invasion in its eastern provinces.

The final onslaught was to come from the Mongols.

*****

CHAPTER EIGHT
The Mongols

The Chinese historian, Sima Qian (145-86 BCE), was probably the first to record the existence of nomadic tribes living in the region of today's Mongolia. However, the first specific mention of the term Mongols came during the Tang dynasty in 8th Century China. By the 13th Century, the word Mongols had become an umbrella term to describe all the tribes that had been united under Genghis Khan, who founded the Mongol Empire. Eventually, ethnic Mongols would hold the titles of Emperor of China, Padishah of Persia, Sultan of Egypt, Sultan of the Golden Horde, as well as Great Khan of the Mongols.

We get most of our information about the Mongols from *The Secret History of the Mongols*, which was written following the death of Genghis Khan in 1227. The original work, which has not survived, was written in the Mongol script. The Mongolian text was translated into Chinese and it is these translations that have survived until today.

Before the rise of Genghis Khan, the steppe region of Mongolia, an area the size of France, Germany, Italy and the UK combined, was inhabited by pastoral nomadic tribes who measured their wealth in people and livestock, rather than territory. Goats, cattle and sheep provided meat and milk as well as wool and leather for clothing and felt was used for circular tents, or *gers*. The Mongols used camels for transporting goods, but their most prized possession was the short Mongolian horse. All male and female members of the clan or tribe were trained in hunting and horsemanship from a very early age, and at times of war, these same skills were easily transferrable to the battle-field.

The tribes had to move to new pastures each season, which frequently brought them into conflict as each tribe competed for grazing land. At times of inter-tribal warfare, apart from seizing livestock, it was commonplace for women to be stolen as wives. Orphans were also seized, and adopted by new families as a way of increasing the size of the tribe. Peace between the tribes was usually achieved through a political alliance, a blood-brother alliance, or an arranged marriage. But as fast as these alliances were made, they were broken.

Genghis Khan: 1162-1227

Genghis (also spelt Chinggis, Chingis, Jenghiz, Jinghis) Khan was born in 1162 in the Kentii Mountain region of north-eastern Mongolia. The area of his birth was rich in iron and it was known for the manufacture of weaponry as well as stirrups, which were only used by senior members of the tribe. Genghis's birth name was Temujin; 'temu', meaning iron and Temujin meaning iron-worker, or blacksmith. It is traditionally believed that he was named after a Tatar warrior who had been captured by his father.

Temujin was the first son of Yesugei, leader of the Borijin clan. The Borijin was a senior clan within the Mongol hierarchy and Temujin's father was a grandson of Khabul Khan, a direct descendent of Batichikan, the founder of the Mongols.

Early in his life, Temujin fell victim to tribal warfare. Together with his mother and siblings, he was rejected by his tribe and with no clan protection, the family spent several years on the steppe, surviving on wild fruits and small game. On another occasion his young bride was stolen, and he was also captured and enslaved by a rival tribe. These early experiences, as well as the resourcefulness of his mother Hoelun, were to influence Genghis throughout his life. Crucially, he came to believe that the only way that the Mongols could progress was to learn to live in peace among themselves and cease inter-tribal warfare. In other words, they had to unite.

Temujin first allied with Togrul, Khan of the Keraites, a tribe that had a large Christian Nestorian population. Together they were able to subdue other rival tribes, including the Naimans and the Merkits, the tribe that had stolen his bride. In 1186, Temujin was elected Khan of the Khamag Mongol and in 1206, having subdued even more tribes, he was elected 'Great Khan', better known in the West as Genghis Khan. As Great Khan he was bestowed with the Mandate of Tengri, or the Mandate of the

'Eternal Blue Sky'. This is similar to the Chinese tradition, where Emperors were awarded the Mandate of Heaven, but in the case of the Mongolians, the mandate included the ceremonial affirmation of the Shaman, whose role was to communicate between the Eternal Blue Sky and people on earth.

To be eligible for election, a Great Khan had to satisfy two criteria: first, proven military success, and second, evidence of the ability to withstand hardship. It was believed that only those who had suffered themselves, would be able to understand the needs of their men and therefore provide good leadership. Genghis Khan fulfilled both of these criteria.

His military success was partly due to his innovative policies that eventually came to be incorporated into the *Yasa,* or Mongol Law. Since his aim was to end tribal warfare, Genghis put men from different clans together rather than have units made up of the same clan or tribe. In this way he weakened tribal loyalty, while strengthening loyalty to himself. It was a policy not dissimilar to that adopted by the Ottomans when they captured young Christian boys from the Balkans to train as Janissaries. In the case of the Ottomans, the intention was to replace loyalty to home and family, with loyalty to the Sultan and Janissary Corps.

Another key feature was to break with tradition by appointing his generals according to merit rather than on a hereditary basis. And he increased his fighting force by incorporating male prisoners into his army, and especially prisoners who were skilled in engineering or siege warfare. Genghis also believed that to win in battle, it was necessary to understand what motivated the enemy and he therefore maintained a vast network of spies. He had a reputation for valuing loyalty above all else and was ruthless towards those who defied him, whether it be a member of his own family, his own clan, or a rebellious vassal state.

Expansion of the Mongol Empire

By 1206, Genghis Khan had succeeded in uniting all the Mongol tribes under his authority. But just as the Rashidun had experienced in the 7th Century (see Chapter 6), peace among the tribes resulted in a loss of income due to the prohibition regarding looting within the tribal federation. For both the Rashidun and the Mongols, the answer was to invade territory further afield.

As early as 1205, Temujin was conducting raids into the Tangut territory of the Chinese Western Xia, a region that straddles today's Northwest China, Northeast Tibet and Southern Mongolia. Then, in 1209, he prepared for a full-scale invasion. Having no siege engines, his tactic was to cut the water supplies to the capital city of Yinchuan. Despite the fact that his own camp was flooded in the process, in January 1210, the Western Xia surrendered and became a vassal of the Mongols. As a mark of loyalty, the Tangut Emperor Li Anquan, gave his daughter in marriage to the Great Khan.

For decades the Jin dynasty of China had terrorized the Mongol tribes of the steppe by demanding exorbitant tribute and often capturing and enslaving the people. On one occasion, Emperor Xizong of the Jin ordered the crucifixion of Ambaghai, Khan of the Kamag Mongol. In 1210, when the new Jin Emperor, Wanyan Yongji, demanded the submission of the Mongols, Genghis Khan reportedly spat on the ground in disdain. Such an act was tantamount to a declaration of war.

In August 1211, the first of what became known as the Mongol-Jin Wars took place at the Battle of Yehuling in the Hebei Province of today's China. The result was a resounding victory for the Mongols and the loss of thousands of Jin troops. Five years later, with the help of defecting Han troops and the Ongut tribes, Genghis seized the city of Zhongdu (today's Beijing). The Onguts were Nestorian Christians and under the vassalage of the Jin, their task had been to guard the Great Wall. On this occasion, the Onguts sided with the Mongols and showed them a safe passage into Jin territory. Faced with the onslaught of the Mongols, the Jin abandoned the city of Zhongdu and consequently they were forced to move their capital to Kaifeng in the South.

Having defeated the Jin, the Mongols gained immense wealth.

Apart from territory and tribute, the Great Khan now had access to engineers experienced in siege warfare, Chinese explosives, skilled artisans, scholars, doctors, musicians and merchants.

The next state to fall to the Mongols, in 1218, was the khanate of the Qara Khitai, a dynasty that had ruled a large part of Central Asia for almost a hundred years. By gaining the submission of the Qara Khitai, the Mongol Empire now stretched as far west as Lake Balkhash, which bordered the Khwarezmian Empire.

Conquest of the Khwarezmian Empire

At that time, the Khwarezmians ruled an area that roughly equated to today's Iran, Uzbekistan, Turkmenistan and Tajikistan. The population was largely a mix of Persian peasants and merchants, while Turks represented the warrior and ruling class. The Empire was ruled by Shah Muhammad II of Khwarazm, who was unpopular with many of his subjects, particularly those who had only recently been subjugated and incorporated into his Empire.

Most importantly, Khwarezmia included a large stretch of the Silk Road, including the wealthy cities of Samarkand, Bukhara and Urgench, which were all in today's Uzbekistan and Merv, in modern Turkmenistan. Genghis Khan believed that trade with the Khwarezmians could provide income to help pay for his growing army. Hoping to secure a trade deal with the ruler, Genghis sent a delegation to meet the Shah in Samarkand. But the caravan carrying the delegates was intercepted by Inalchuq, governor of the city of Otrar, who suspected the presence of spies. Inachuq executed most of the Mongols and seized their goods. A second, smaller, delegation succeeded in gaining an audience with the Shah. But once more the Mongols were humiliated. One member of the delegation was beheaded by the Shah and he sent the head of the dead man back to the Great Khan.

It is generally accepted that Genghis Khan had never intended to conquer the Kharezmian Empire. He was simply motivated by a desire for trade. But after such humiliation, followed by several days praying to Tengri, the Great God of the Sky, for guidance, he decided to take his revenge.

In 1219, Genghis ordered his son Jochi, together with his general Jebe, to advance with an army of around 20,000 men, into the fertile Ferghana Valley and destroy all in their path. At the same time, another force of some 60,000, led by two of Genghis's other sons, Chagatai and Ogedei, besieged the city of Otrar. The defenders held out for five months. The siege was finally broken when a traitor opened the gate for the Mongols. Streets were flattened to make way for the Mongol cavalry and remaining houses were burnt to the ground. Some reports claim that the governor, Inalchuq, was then executed by having molten silver poured into his eyes and ears.

Because the city had refused to submit, the majority of the population was massacred. An exception was made for artisans, who were sent back to Mongolia, where their skills would be put to good use. Young women and boys were also spared and either sold into slavery or given away to his troops as slaves. Some young men were forced into the Mongol army and often used as cannon fodder. They would be forced to march in front of the advancing army, clearing roads or digging ditches or simply being the first to face enemy fire as human shields. This was a pattern that the Mongols would use repeatedly in their marches of conquest.

In 1220, Genghis made for the city of Bukhara, which at that time was an important trading city and the cultural centre of the Eastern Islamic world. After a fifteen-day siege the city surrendered. It is said that Genghis made straight for the Grand Mosque, thinking that it was a palace. When the citizens gathered, he ordered them to bring fodder for his horses and he then proceeded to feed them in the mosque which was an act of sacrilege in the eyes of the Muslim faithful.

The next city to be conquered was Samarkand, the capital of the empire and seat of Shah Muhammad who had already fled with his family. After negotiations with the elders, Genghis agreed to spare the lives of 50,000 citizens in exchange for agreeing to open the gates.

From Samarkand, the Mongol troops advanced to Urgench, which was another wealthy trading city. Genghis had promised Urgench to his eldest son Jochi once it had been taken. However, the battle for Urgench proved to be the most difficult of all the Central Asian cities to conquer. Being built along the river Amu Darya, the land was marshy, which made siege warfare difficult. Furthermore, the citizens put up a good fight and the Mongols were forced into hand-to-hand street fighting. Being more used to fighting on the move from their swift horses, they found themselves at a disadvantage. Their problems were further exacerbated by disagreements among the brothers. While Jochi wanted to keep as much of the city intact, since it was to be his inheritance, Chagatai favoured the usual Mongol tactic of laying it waste. Genghis settled the matter by putting his other son, Ogedei, in charge. According to the Persian historian Juvayni, over a million citizens of Urgench were executed, making it one of the bloodiest massacres in history.

It was around this time that Genghis Khan nominated his son Ogedei to succeed him as Great Khan. Then, having conquered the Khwarazmian Empire, Genghis sent his generals Jebe and Subutai further West into the Caucasus. They invaded Georgia, Armenia, Azerbaijan, Crimea, Kievan Rus and Volga Bulgaria. In 1225, the generals returned to Mongolia. They had acquired valuable information about the political and cultural life of the Eurasian steppe. Above all, the region north of the Danube contained rich pastures that the Mongols envisaged as ripe for future conquest.

As the Mongol conquest moved further West, the people of Europe were beginning to hear about these warlike invaders from the East. It was even speculated that Genghis Khan might have been the fabled Prester John, thought by some to be the ruler of the Eastern Nestorian Church, or King David of India. It was reported that in 1221, the Latin Bishop of Acre had received news that an army from the East was sweeping across Central Asia, conquering Islamic lands in the process. The army was heading towards Baghdad and Christians in the Levant hoped that Prester John would eventually liberate Jerusalem following its reconquest by Saladin in 1187. Since Genghis had always taken a very tolerant attitude towards Christians, and had Christian wives, the theory is not entirely without foundation.

Genghis Khan's last years

While his generals were invading the Caucasus, Genghis led the main army through Afghanistan towards Mongolia. Once he had gathered all his forces together, Genghis planned to deal with some unfinished business in China. When he had earlier turned his attention to the Khwarezmia Empire in the west, he had asked the Tanguts, who were his vassals, to join him in the conquest. Not only did the Tanguts refuse, but they allied with the Chinese Jin and Song dynasties against the Mongols. Now, Genghis's response to this act of disloyalty was brutal. He ordered the systematic destruction of all Tangut cities and farmland, as well as the massacre of civilians.

In 1225, with an army of 180,000 the Mongols swept into the Tangut territory of Western Xia destroying all garrisons, cities and towns in his wake. It is estimated that by the time the capital city of Yinchuan finally fell in 1227, some six million Tangut had died. The result was the annihilation of the Tangut people. According to John Man (*Genghis Khan: life, death and resurrection,* 2005), this was possibly the first case of systematic genocide in history.

Genghis Khan had reaped his revenge but he had died in the process. The exact cause of his death is clouded in mystery, other than it happened during the battle for Yinchuan in August 1227. He was 64 years old and it is possible that he died from war injuries or fell from his horse. His body was taken for burial at his birth place in the Kentii Mountains. The exact location was kept a secret.

Yasa Law

A lasting legacy of Genghis Khan was the *Yasa* (*Yassa*), or Mongol Law. While initially established within the context of the Great Khan's military campaigns, the *Yasa* eventually came to encompass all aspects of Mongol life. It was originally written in the Uighur script and because it was only accessible to Genghis and his immediate family, it has been called the 'Secret Law'. However, no complete copy has survived and the only information we have on its content has been pieced together from surviving portions.

As Genghis Khan conquered and consolidated his empire, his laws extended beyond the military, and into domestic law. His intention was to eradicate the ills that he had beset his own early life. One of his first laws was to forbid the kidnapping or selling of wives. He also attacked illegitimacy by declaring that all children, including children of concubines and orphans, should be legally adopted by a family. And he laid down strict regulations regarding theft. For example, if a lost animal, or other piece of property was found, and not returned to its owner, that was considered theft.

The *Yasa* covered rules regarding war and dealing with the enemy, including pillage and the treatment of prisoners. It dictated how to host the stranger and covered personal hygiene as well as how to wash clothes. Interestingly, at a time of religious intolerance in the Christian West, the *Yasa* demanded that people should enjoy complete freedom of religion to people within his empire as long as they obeyed the *Yasa* law.

Sorghaghtani Beki, the Mongol Empress

Just before Genghis died in, 1227, he divided the Mongol Empire between his four sons. Jochi, the eldest, received territory in the northeast of what was Russia. But since Jochi died a few months before Genghis, his territory was further divided into khanates that eventually became known as the Golden Horde. Chagatai, the second son, was given the region of Central Asia and Northern Iran, which became known as the Chagatai Khanate. Ogedei, the third son, succeeded Genghis as the Great Khan and inherited the eastern part of the Empire including China, which would later become the Yuan Dynasty ruled by Kublai Khan. The fourth son, Tolui, inherited the smallest region of the Mongol homeland.

Tolui married Sorghaghtani Beki, who was a Keraite princess

and in common with many Keraites, she was a Nestorian Christian. It was even rumoured that she might have been a daughter of the fabled Prester John.

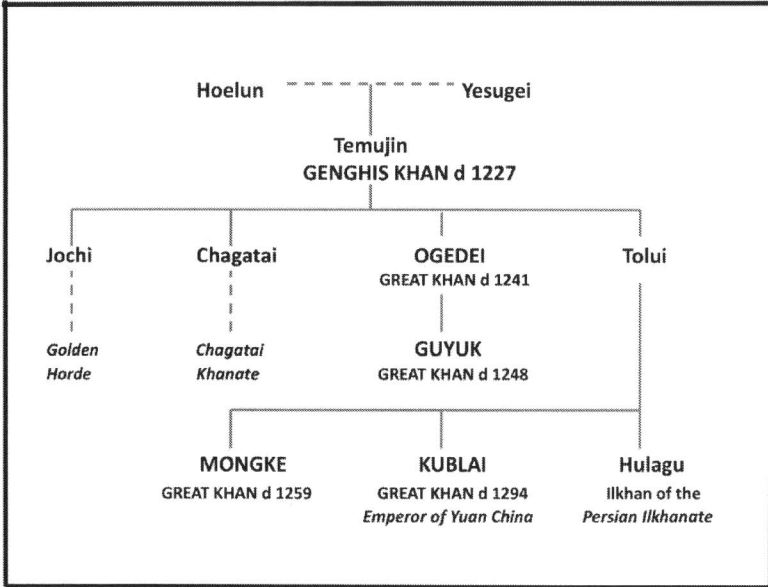

```
        Hoelun  -------- Yesugei
                    |
                Temujin
            GENGHIS KHAN d 1227
                    |
   _____
   |          |             |              |
 Jochi    Chagatai       OGEDEI          Tolui
                      GREAT KHAN d 1241
   |          |             |              |
 Golden    Chagatai       GUYUK
 Horde     Khanate     GREAT KHAN d 1248
                    _____
                    |             |             |
                 MONGKE        KUBLAI        Hulagu
            GREAT KHAN d 1259  GREAT KHAN d 1294  Ilkhan of the
                          Emperor of Yuan China  Persian Ilkhanate
```

Mongol women at that time enjoyed a greater freedom than those of most other cultures. From childhood, they learned to hunt and fight alongside their brothers, but in the realm of the home they were particularly powerful, partly because the men could be away for many months at a time. Although Sorghaghtani was illiterate, she understood the importance of education for her sons. Consequently, she ensured that they received not only the best education, but also became proficient in foreign languages that would be necessary if they were to be successful in the further expansion of the Mongol domains.

When Tolui died at the early age of 41, Ogedei, the Great Khan proposed marriage to Sorghaghtani. But when she declined, he decreed that all of Tolui's lands should come under her rule. From this moment on, Sorghaghtani became the second most powerful person among the Mongols and Ogedei the Great Khan frequently consulted with her on important matters of state. She handled all matters of administration and was largely instrumental for creating the *Pax Mongolia*, which was a time of relative peace across Central and Eastern Asia. Under her rule, the cities of the Silk Road came under one administration which eased travel between East and West. With easier and safer travel along the Silk Road, a new generation of Europeans, such as Marco Polo, were able to make the journey to the East.

Sorghaghtani died in 1252 at the age of 62 and was buried in a Christian church. She was viewed as an Empress among the Mongols and is spoken highly of by Christian, Muslim and Chinese historians. According to the Persian historian Rashid-al-Din Hamadani, she was '*Extremely intelligent and able...the most intelligent woman in the world. There is no doubt that it was through her intelligence and ability that she raised the station of her sons above that of their cousins and caused them to attain to the rank of qa'ans and emperors*'.

Three of Sorghaghtani's sons did indeed go on to become emperors or great khans in their own right. The two eldest, Mongke and Kublai, became Great Khan in succession, with Kublai simultaneously holding the title of Emperor of China. The third son, Hulagu, became Ilkhan of the Persian Ilkhanate which was the forerunner of the Safavid Dynasty, followed by the country of modern Iran.

Hulagu and the Siege of Baghdad, 1258

In 1255, Hulagu was commissioned by his brother Mongke, the Great Khan, to gain the submission of, or conquer, all Islamic lands in southwest Asia. These included the Nizari Ismailis and especially their Assassin hideout of Alamut (see Chapter Seven), the Abbasids in Baghdad, the Ayyubids in Syria and the Mamluks in Egypt. Controversy remains over whether or not Mongke ordered Hulagu to overthrow the Abbasid Caliphate, or simply gain its submission, together with a troop levy.

In preparation for the campaign, one tenth of all fighting men throughout the Mongol Empire were conscripted to Hulagu's army, which was then complemented by troops from the Christian kingdoms of Armenia, Georgia and the Frankish crusader kingdom of Antioch, all of which viewed the Islamic world as enemy territory. With the addition of a further 1,000 Chinese artillery experts and sappers, the total number made it perhaps the largest Mongol army ever assembled.

Hulagu's first target was the Assassin fortress of Alamut. As early as 1253, Kitbuqa Noyan, who was a Nestorian Christian of the Naiman tribe, and a general in Hulagu's army, had attempted to eradicate the Assassins in response to their repeated attacks on the Mongols. However, in 1256, the Assassins finally surrendered to Hulagu's vast army. The Grand Master was executed, the fortress destroyed and the majority of the surviving Assassins sought refuge in Syria.

Hulagu's next move was to send a message to Al-Musta'sim, the Caliph of the Abbasids, setting out the terms of submission demanded by Mongke. When these were rejected by the Caliph, Hulagu began his march towards Baghdad, the capital of the Abbasids and the symbolic centre of the Islamic world.

By the middle of January, 1258, Hulagu's army was camped on both sides of the Tigris on the outskirts of Baghdad. Neither the Ayyubids of Syria nor the Mamluks of Egypt were in a position to come to the aid of Baghdad because both powers were preparing their own defense against the advancing Mongols. The Abbasids were totally unprepared for the onslaught. Compared to the Mongols, their army was ill-equipped and undisciplined. The only option left to the Caliph was to mount a cavalry force of 20,000 but this was quickly wiped out.

On the 29th January, with the aid of siege engines and catapults, the Mongols laid siege to the city. By the 5th February, the walls had been breached. Attempts by the Caliph and his senior advisers to negotiate with Hulagu failed and on the 10th February, the city finally surrendered.

What followed was a disaster, not only for Baghdad and the Abbasid Caliphate, but for the whole Islamic world. After being forced to watch his citizens being massacred, Al-Musta'sim was executed by being rolled in a blanket and trampled on by horses. The number of men, women and children killed by Hulagu's forces were said to be anywhere from 90,000 to two million. But the greatest non-human catastrophe was the destruction of so much Islamic cultural heritage for which Baghdad was famous.

Mosques, libraries and academic institutions were completely destroyed. The famous House of Wisdom, also known as the Grand Library of Baghdad, was burnt to the ground and its most precious collection of books, dating back to the 8th Century, was thrown into the Tigris. Not only had the Grand Library provided a place of study for some of the greatest Islamic scholars, but the institution had been the primary centre for the translation of works on philosophy, medicine, mathematics, science and astronomy, from the Greek language into Arabic.

Not only was the city of Baghdad virtually depopulated by Hulagu's troops, but the canals, which for centuries had provided vital irrigation, were also destroyed. This was to have a disastrous effect on agriculture in the area for many years to come.

Hulagu's Christian wife successfully pleaded for the lives of the Christians of Baghdad to be spared. Consequently, the Caliph's palace was given to the Nestorian Catholicos, who then went on to build a cathedral.

The sacking of Baghdad has been seen by historians as marking the end of the 'golden age' of Islam. It was certainly a watershed in Islamic history and it marked a shift in the symbolic importance of the Caliphate from Baghdad to Cairo.

Decline of the Mongols

Having defeated the Abbasids, Hulagu turned his attention to Syria where the Ayyubids held power. His allied force, that now included Christians from Cilicia, first captured Aleppo. By March 1260, they had also taken Damascus, where a Christian mass was held in the historic Umayyad mosque.

Hulagu's next target was to be the Mamluk dynasty in Cairo. However, because the Levant produced insufficient fodder for his horses, he moved the bulk of his army back into Azerbaijan for the summer months, leaving behind a small force of 20,000 under the leadership of his general Kitquba. Hulagu then had to return to Mongolia in order to attend the *kurultai*, the traditional succession council following the death of his brother Mongke Khan.

When the Mamluk Sultan Qutuz realized how few Mongols remained in the Levant, he seized the opportunity to attack them with his own well-equipped and well-disciplined force. He was also joined by another Mamluk leader named Baibars, who had been in Damascus when the city fell to the Mongols. Faced with the threat from the Mamluks, Kitquba attempted an alliance with the Christian Crusader kingdom of Jerusalem, which at that time was based in Acre. But he was thwarted by the fact that such a Franco-Mongol alliance had been forbidden by the Pope.

Although the Mamluks were traditional enemies of the Crusader kingdoms, they permitted the Sultan's troops to march unmolested northwards through their territory towards Acre. At the same time, the Mongols were marching southwards from Damascus. The two armies met in the September of 1260 and engaged at the Battle of Ain Jalut, in southeast Galilee near Nazareth. After many hours of hard combat, the Mamluks, largely under the leadership of Baibars, won the day. It was to be the first serious defeat that the Mongols had suffered and marked the end of their campaigns of expansion beyond Syria.

Baibars would later turn his attention to the Crusader Kingdom of Jerusalem. He commissioned the Assassins to kill Philip of Montfort and he captured the crusader castles of Montfort and Krak des Chevaliers in Syria. In 1291 his grandson, al-Ashraf Khalil, instigated the fall of the last Crusader Kingdom in Acre, which marked the demise of the Crusader presence in the Levant.

Conclusion

There is no doubt that the Mongol invasions sent shockwaves throughout the regions they conquered, whether that be southwards into China, or westwards across Central Asia into Europe and the Levant. Furthermore, they were shockwaves that would change the face of huge swathes of Asia and leave a lasting economic, political and cultural legacy.

Historians, both Eastern and Western, have generally portrayed the Mongols in a negative light. They have been described as barbaric warlords who ravaged lands, burnt cities to the ground, raped, massacred and enslaved millions of innocent people. Perhaps the greatest example of Mongol atrocity was the sacking of Baghdad by Genghis's grandson Hulagu in 1260, which historians mark as ending the Golden Age of Islam. It has since been debated as to whether or not the Great Khan had intended the total destruction of the Caliphate, or simply its submission. Whatever the truth may have been, Hulagu decided to sack the city, murder the Caliph and murder or enslave most of the citizens. It is estimated that the Iranian plateau lost three quarters of its population due to Mongol invasions and the region did not begin to fully recover until the middle of the 20th Century.

While it is true that the Mongols can be accused of brutality and atrocity on a vast scale, they may not necessarily have been any worse than other powers of the time. Furthermore, it is worth considering two other points. First, how was it possible for a single nomad, who had struggled for survival in his early life, to come to rule one of the largest empires in the world? Second, the legacy of their many positive achievements deserves recognition.

Regarding the meteoric rise of the young Temujin, to become leader of a huge empire, it is clear that he was both politically astute and a skillful military tactician. His childhood experiences of rejection, kidnap and above all, survival on the steppe under the guidance of his mother, made him aware of the many problems existing at the time in Mongol culture. He also learnt to respect the advice of his mother which is an example of the influence that women held in Mongol society. Tolui's wife, Sorghaghtani Beki, was another example of a powerful and extremely influential woman.

Throughout his rule, Genghis aimed to unite the Mongol tribes under his sole rule. By way of alliances and the submission of vassal states, he grew his empire. He then insisted on absolute loyalty and any who denied his authority, whether family, friend, clan or state, would suffer his wrath. The Tanguts of Western Xia, learned this to their cost. When they refused to join Genghis on his campaign to Khwarezmia, he responded by nothing less than an act of genocide.

As a military tactician, Genghis adopted methods that were unique for the time. The two most significant were: first, to put troops from the same tribe into different units, so replacing tribal loyalty with loyalty to himself and second, to appoint according to merit rather than on a hereditary basis. His military innovations and rules for civil and domestic life, were later enshrined into the *Yasa*, or Mongol Law.

Although the Mongols, both men and women, were skilled fighters in the saddle, Genghis was aware of the many short-comings of his military capability during the early years. He therefore wisely made sure that no enemy soldiers, who were expert in military, and especially siege, warfare were killed. Rather, he brought them into his own ranks. When he conquered the Chinese Jin dynasty, for example, he acquired not only military expertise and hardware, but also the service of doctors, scientists and scholars. Indeed, northern Chinese generals, engineers and sappers, would play a key role in his later campaigns.

One of the great achievements of the Mongol period was the unification of the Silk Road, which is symbolized by the *Pax Mongolia*. For the first time in its history, the Silk Road came under one central power. This enabled the standardization of road taxes, staging posts and above all, security. Consequently, travel between China and the Mediterranean ensured far greater safety than previously and apart from the flow of goods, a new generation of travelers, adventurers and missionaries set off for the East.

It is sometimes assumed that the Mongols were religiously intolerant. Certainly, during the reigns of Genghis Khan and his immediate successors, this was not the case. On the contrary, the Great Khan promoted the freedom of religion, a doctrine that

126

became enshrined within the *Yasa* Law, but conditional upon absolute adherence to the *Yasa*. Several Mongol vassal states were Christian, for example, the Onguts and Keraites, and intermarriage between Mongols, Christians and Buddhists was common-place.

While the Battle of Ain Jalut in Galilee in 1260 marked the end of Mongol expansion in the West, the Mongol presence in Russia under the Golden Horde, and in China under the Yuan Dynasty, continued for several more centuries, In Central Asia, the next great leader of Turco-Mongol descent would be Timur, known in the West as Tamerlane.

*****

CHAPTER NINE

From Tamerlane to Nader Shah: 1265-1747

The Ilkhanate that had been ruled by Hulagu and his successors, lasted from 1256 until 1335. At the height of its power, the Khanate had ruled over an area that included parts of today's Iraq, Iran, Georgia, Turkmenistan, Afghanistan and Tajikistan. During this time, the majority of the population converted to Islam, while the Ilkhanate Court retained Tengrist, Buddhist or Nestorian affiliation.

The death in 1335 of Abu Sa'id Bahadur, the last Khan of the House of Hulagu, led to a series of civil wars among the various pretenders to the throne. At the same time, there was growing conflict between the Ilkhanate, which remained loyal to the Great Khan, and the Golden Horde, the Mongol state that ruled large parts of Russia.

But perhaps the greatest cause that led to the downfall of the Ilkhanate, was the Black Death. Thought to have originated on the plains of Central Asia, the disease-bearing rats travelled along the Silk Road to Constantinople, where they managed to get on ships destined for ports throughout Europe. Among the many thousands of casualties along the Silk Road were two of the Ilkhanate Khan's sons.

With the demise of the Ilkhanate, much of the region broke away into independent khanates, while other areas were absorbed into the growing Ottoman Empire.

Timur, the Sword of Islam: 1336-1405

The next great conqueror to rise in Central Asia was the Turco-Mongol warlord Timur, historically known as Amir Timur, or Timur Gurkani (Gurkani meaning 'son-in-law' of the Genghisids). He also described himself as the 'Sword of Islam', reflecting the fact that he used Islamic symbols throughout his period of conquest. In the West, Timur was known as Tamerlane, which is derived from 'Timur the Lame' on account of his limp. The traditional account is that Timur was shot by an arrow in the leg while hunting as a youth. However, there is an alternative theory that he received an injury to his leg and lost two fingers as an adult, when fighting as a mercenary.

Timur was born in 1336 in the town of Kesh, near today's Samarkand in Uzbekistan, which was then part of the Chagatai Khanate. Although the population was largely Turco-Mongol, the people no longer followed a nomadic life-style and could be described as Islamic-Iranian, but influenced by Persian culture.

Throughout his life, Timur's hero and role-model had been Genghis Khan. Furthermore, his long-held ambition was to bring all territory that had once been conquered by Genghis, into a restored and reunited Mongol empire. To this end, part of his strategy was to claim descent from the Great Khan. However, this was not straight-forward because Timur belonged to the Barlas clan, while Genghis was from the Borijin clan. To get around the problem, he claimed the common ancestry of both clans to Tumanay Khan. His claim was further strengthened through his own marriage to Saray Mulk Khanum. She became his chief consort but crucially she was a member of the Borijin clan and therefore a direct descendent of Genghis. In other words, Timur claimed his legitimacy on the grounds of a common ancestry and through marriage, hence the term 'Gurkani', son-in-law.

By the time Timur was 24, he was beginning to make a name for himself as a military leader, He joined forces with Qazaghan, the Khan of the Chagatai Khanate and between them, they invaded Khorasan, which straddled parts of today's Iran, Afghanistan and Central Asia. They also subdued Khwarezm, which included parts of today's Uzbekistan, Kazakhstan and Turkmenistan. Following the assassination of Qazaghan, Timur acquired the whole region of Transoxania and at about the same time, on the death of his father, he became Amir of the Barlas clan.

The Rise of the Timurid Empire 1370-1507

By 1370, Timur ruled over vast swathes of the eastern part of Central Asia. When politically expedient, and to strengthen his legitimacy, he nominated 'puppet' khans from the Borijin clan, to rule in his name. Having consolidated his power in the East, he then turned his attention to the successor states of the Ilkhanate in the West. By 1390, he had conquered Isfahan and Shiraz in today's Iran, and reached as far as Baghdad in modern Iraq.

His next challenge was the Golden Horde, sometimes referred to as the Kipchak Khanate, or the Ulus of Jochi. At the height of its power the Golden Horde ruled an area extending from the River Danube and the Urals in the West, to Siberia in the East and it stretched southwards to the Black Sea and the Caucasus.

The Golden Horde was made up of different 'wings', and in 1380, conflict broke out between the two most important; the Blue Horde and the White Horde. Tokhtamysh, a direct descendent of Genghis Khan, and leader of the Blue Horde, sought refuge with Timur in Samarkand. With the help of Timur, Tokhtamysh was then able to overthrow the White Horde and for a short time the Golden Horde was reunited.

However, in 1389, Tokhtamysh turned against his ally and he attacked Timur's territory in Transoxania. This resulted in two fierce battles between the Golden Horde and the Timurids. Timur finally defeated Tokhtamysh in 1395 at the Battle of the Terek River. He then destroyed all the major cities of the Horde, including Sarai, their capital. The defeat of the Golden Horde resulted in Timur's first victims in Western Europe and it also heralded the decline of Mongol rule in Russia.

Having defeated the Golden Horde, thereby extending his territory in the West, Timur then turned eastwards and invaded the region of today's Pakistan and North India. He removed the ruler of the Tughlaq dynasty of Delhi and appointed Khizr Khan as governor, so establishing the Sayyid Dynasty of Delhi, which was to last until 1450 as a vassal state of the Timurids.

The Timurid-Ottoman Wars

The most serious threat to the growing power of the Timurids at the time came from the Ottomans. In 1402, the Ottoman Sultan Bayezid I, nick-named 'lightening, or thunderbolt', on account of his swift and successful campaigns, demanded tribute from one of Timur's loyal emirs. This was an affront to Timur and the incident eventually resulted in open warfare.

On the 28th July 1402, the two armies met at the Battle of Ankara, in today's Turkey. Timur's army numbered approximately 140,000, including a large number of war elephants. Bayezid's smaller force, of some 85,000, included his Janissaries and troops from the Ottoman vassal states. Key among the vassals was the Prince of Serbia, Stefan Lazarevic, known as 'Stefan the Tall'. Lazarevic had a reputation for being one of the greatest knights of the time and Timur was impressed with his bravery on the battle field.

During the battle, Timur cut off the water supply to the Ottoman forces, which left them in a weak position. Another blow for the Ottomans was the defection of some of their Tatar vassals to Timur. The result was a victory for the Timurids. Bayezid was captured by Timur and he died while still in captivity the following year.

The death of Bayezid resulted in a succession crisis, as four of his sons fought for the throne. Civil war, known as the Ottoman Interregnum, raged for almost eleven years, until finally one son, Mehmed Celebi, emerged as victor. In July 1413, he crowned himself Sultan Mehmed I.

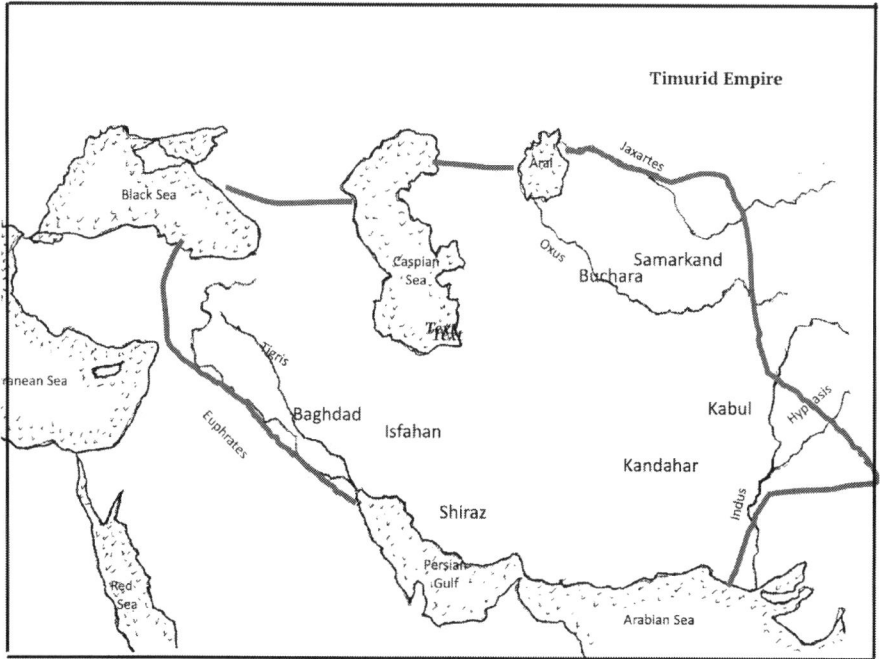

Timurid Empire

The Siege of Smyrna and the Knights of Rhodes, 1402

Following the Battle of Ankara, Timur advanced towards the city of Smyrna, which is modern-day Izmir, on the Anatolian coast. Since its capture by the Western Crusaders in 1344, the city had been under the jurisdiction of the Papacy in Rome. In 1374, it was put under the protection of the Knights of Rhodes, also known as the Knights Hospitallers.

In order to protect the city, the Knights, numbering around 200, built a fortified castle at the entrance to the harbour. As Timur's forces approached, the Knights dug a deep ditch to separate the castle from the mainland. While ships arrived by sea with extra munitions, reinforcements and supplies, many local Christians fled the city.

Hoping to avoid the costs of a siege, Timur offered to spare the city if the Knights either converted to Islam or accepted vassalage. When the Knights rejected the terms, Timur prepared to attack. On the 2nd December 1402, his forces began bombarding the walls and filling in the ditch so that his siege engines could reach the walls. He also tried to block the harbour. The walls of the castle were soon breached. Those Knights who could, escaped by ship, while the inhabitants within the castle were all massacred. According to some accounts, the Timurids used decapitated heads as projectiles against Crusader ships and galleys that were moored in the harbour.

Overall, the siege lasted about fifteen days and it was in the context of this battle against the Christian Knights that Timur referred to himself as the 'Sword of Islam'. After defeating the Knights, Timur destroyed the sea-castle, but he reinforced the mainland city of Smyrna. The Grand Master of the Knights, Philibert de Naillac, managed to escape to the ancient city of Halicarnassus further along the coast, where he built another fortified castle. Now known as Bodrum, the remains of the castle can still be seen today.

From Anatolia, Timur returned to Samarkand. His intention was to prepare a campaign against Ming China. While he would normally wait until Spring before setting off on campaign, this time he decided to leave in the December of 1404. But he failed to reach the Chinese border. In February 1405, he died of an illness while camped at Otrar, in today's Kazakhstan.

The Timurid Renaissance

Timur ruled for a total of 35 years, during which time he was never once defeated in battle. Recognised as one of the greatest military tacticians in history, he was also responsible for the deaths of some 17 million people. He achieved his ambition to retake and reunite those lands that had previously been conquered by Genghis Khan, but unlike the Great Khan, Timur campaigned in the name of Islam, referring to himself as 'The Sword of Islam'.

Timur also differed from Genghis Khan in another way. Genghis remained close to his nomadic Mongol roots. While he conquered huge swathes of Central and Eastern Asia, he was only interested in filling his coffers with pillage, acquiring slaves and creating vassal states that provided tribute. Timur, on the other hand, wanted to build an empire of great cities comparable with other empires of the time. Whenever he was on campaign, he picked the most skilled architects and engineers from among his prisoners and sent them back to Transoxania to work on his building projects. The most significant city to be created by Timur was his capital, Samarkand, which had previously been destroyed by Genghis Khan. Under the Timurids, Herat and Bukhara also became important centres of Islamic culture.

The period between the late 14th Century and early 16th Century, is often referred to as the Timurid Renaissance. It began at the end of the Mongol invasions and it coincided with the European Renaissance. During this time, there was a creative synthesis of Mongol, Persian, Chinese and Seljuk cultures. The Turco-Mongol languages, such as Chaghatai, were used by the military, Persian was the language of Government and the Civil Service and Arabic the language of science and religion.

Timur was an enthusiastic patron of the arts, which were influenced both by Persian and Chinese cultures. Not only did he commission the most skilled architects of the Islamic world to build his palaces, mosques, madrassas and mausoleums, but he also invited some of the greatest scholars and poets of the time to join his academies and grace his court. He is also credited with having introduced Tamerlane Chess, which is similar to modern chess, but has a greater number of squares.

Successive Timurid rulers would continue in the tradition of promoting the arts. Nur ad-Din 'Abd al-Rahman, better known as Jami, a poet, historian and theologian, was born in Herat. He was later invited to teach in the Samarkand academies. And Ulugh Beg, who ruled as Khan between 1447 and 1449, was a renowned astronomer and mathematician in his own right. Under the Timurids, Herat became the centre for manuscript painting, while metalwork, ceramics and jade-carving all reached new heights. The later Ottoman, Safavid and Mughal empires would all inherit elements of Timurid art and culture, as well as benefit from Timurid skills in the manufacture of firearms, hence becoming known as the 'Gunpowder Empires'.

Fall

Timur died in February, 1405. By around 1450, the Empire was in decline, triggered by the Turco-Mongol tradition of dividing territory among surviving sons. Parts of Persia, the Caucasus, Mesopotamia and Anatolia fell to the rising Iranian Safavids. In 1506, Kabul, in today's Afghanistan, fell to Babur who was a Turco-Mongol descendent of Timur. Babur later founded the Mughal Empire, which was to rule large swathes of Northern and Central India from 1526 until 1857, when it was dissolved by the British Raj following the Indian Uprising.

As the Empire began to fragment, various Uzbek nomadic tribes fought for control across Central Asia. In 1505, Muhammad Shaybani Khan, a descendent of Jochi, the eldest son of Genghis Khan, seized Samarkand, followed by Herat. The following year he conquered Bukhara. Since Samarkand was in decline at the time, he decided to make Bukhara capital of the Khanate of Bukhara.

The Khanate of Bukhara: 1506-1785

The Shaybani dynasty was to rule the Khanate of Bukhara for the following ninety years. This was followed by the Janid dynasty, which descended from the Astrakhanids, a Tatar state that originated in modern Astrakhan. Throughout the Shaybani and Janid periods, that lasted from 1506 to 1745, Bukhara remained an important centre of Islamic culture. However, in 1740, the Khanate fell to Nader Shah, the ruler of Persia, and for the next few years Bukhara came under Persian rule.

When Nader Shah died in 1747, the Manghit dynasty came to power. The Manghits had been *ataliqs,* or tutors to the Khan's children and during the period under Nader Shah they had steadily risen to power. Unlike most Central Asian khanates, the Manghits were not descended from Genghis Khan. Consequently, when their ruler, Shah Murad, established the Emirate of Bukhara in 1785, he chose the title Emir rather than Khan, which reflected the fact that the state was to be founded upon Islamic principles rather than Genghisid tradition.

The Emirate of Bukhara: 1785-1920

The Emirate of Bukhara covered an area equivalent to today's Uzbekistan and Tajikistan. It was bordered on the West by the Khanate of Khiva and in the East by the Khanate of Khokand in Fergana. Both of these neighbouring Khanates were Genghisids (successors to Genghis Khan).

In 1868, much of the territory belonging to the Emirate of Bukhara fell to Imperial Russia. This happened in the context of Russia's expansionist policies into Central Asia; a policy that frequently brought the Russians into conflict with the British in India. The period of Russian-British conflict in Central Asia at that time is often referred to as the Great Game (see Chapter 10). In 1873, the entire Emirate of Bukhara became a Russian Protectorate.

Th Khanate of Khiva: 1511-1920

The Khanate of Khiva straddled parts of today's Uzbekistan, Kazakhstan and Turkmenistan. In common with the Khanate of Bukhara, it was ruled by members of the Shaybani dynasty. The population was largely made up of Uzbeks and Turkmen as well as Kazakh nomads. Uzbeks generally lived in the towns and cities while Turkmen made up the peasantry.

Throughout much of its history, Khiva, the capital of the Khanate served as a centre for trade in Persian and Russian slaves. However, when Nader Shah conquered the city in 1740, as part of his Central Asian conquests, it is reported that he freed thousands of Persian slaves.

The Khanate of Khiva became a protectorate of Imperial Russia in 1873 and in 1920, following the Russian Revolution, it was renamed the Khorezm People's Soviet Republic.

The Safavid Empire: 1501-1736

While the eastern part of the Timurid Empire fell to the various Uzbek khanates, the western region was gradually conquered by the Safavid dynasty, which originated in the region of Ardabil, northwest Iran. The Safavids were to be the first native Iranian dynasty since the Sassanian period (224-651 CE) and once established, it was to revitalise trade between East and West.

Being one of the 'Gunpowder Empires', alongside the Ottomans and the Mughals, the Safavid period lasted for over two hundred years and is considered to mark the beginning of modern Iran. It was also a watershed in Islamic history in that Shah Ismail I, the founder, introduced Twelver Shi'a Islam as the official religion of the Empire, a situation that remains to this day in modern Iran.

Ismail I was born in Ardabil in 1487. His ancestry was a mix of Turkmen, Kurd, Pontic Greek and Georgian. On his mother's side, he was descended from the Byzantine Emperor Alexios IV of Trebizond. Ismail's father, Haydar, was the sheikh and Grand Master of the Safaviyya Sufi Order.

Sufism is a mystical movement within Islam that places an emphasis on inner spirituality, asceticism and repetitive prayer. Traditionally, adherents normally join a particular Order under the guidance of a Grand Master. Central to Sufi theology is the importance of the life and teaching of the Prophet Muhammad, the perfect Muslim, as an example for all Muslims to emulate.

Sheikh Haydar, Ismail's father, founded the Qizilbash Sufi Order which had a military, as well as spiritual dimension. In this respect, the Qizilbash could be compared to the military religious orders in the West, such as the Knights Hospitaller and Knights Templar that were both founded during the crusading period. Ismail inherited the role of Grand Master of the Safaviyya Sufi Order from his father and the Qizilbash were to play a leading role in the conquests that led to the founding of the Safavid Empire.

At the time of Ismail's birth, the Aq Qoyunlu, an Oghuz Turkic tribal confederation, ruled most of the region. In 1488, Ismail's father was killed in a battle against the Aq Qoyunlu and the child Ismail was forced to seek refuge in Gilan, near the Caspian Sea. During this time, he became multi-lingual and gained an interest in poetry. Later, under the pen-name *Khatai'l,* he wrote 1,400 verses in the Azerbaijani language, much of it with a political undertone.

In 1500, Ismail returned to Azerbaijan and gathered some 7,000 troops, including the Qizilbash, and marched on Shirvan, a vassal state of the Aq Qoyunlu. By 1502, he had defeated the Aq Qoyunlu and was crowned Shahanshah of Iran, making Tabriz his capital. His first act was to proclaim Twelver Shi'ism as the official religion of his realm. He then forced all Sunnis to convert to Shi'ism, often on pain of death if they refused.

By 1510, Ismail had conquered an area including the whole of Iran, Mesopotamia and Eastern Anatolia. At the Battle of Merv, 17,000 Qizilbash warriors defeated the Uzbeks and Muhammad Shaybani Khan, leader of the Khanate of Bukhara, was captured and killed. Typical of the time, Ismail had his skull made into a bejewelled drinking-cup.

The expansionist policies of the Safavids led to conflict with the neighbouring Sunni Ottoman Empire and for many decades the two powers were locked in warfare, as each competed for control over territory in Mesopotamia and Eastern Anatolia. When the Ottomans briefly occupied Tabriz, following the Battle of Chaldiran in 1514, this was a major blow for Ismail, who until this point appeared invincible. Indeed, he is said to have referred to himself as the *Mahdi*, a saviour figure that is prevalent within Shi'ism, and occasionally within Sunnism. From this point on, the Shah withdrew from active campaigning, retreated to his palace, and indulged in a life of alcohol. He died in 1524 at the relatively early age of 36 and was succeeded by his son Tahmasp I.

Shah Tahmasp I: 1524-1576

As with his father, Tahmasp was a minor when he came to the throne. The regency was therefore placed in the hands of the powerful Qizilbash who constantly fought among themselves for the leadership. Consequently, when Tahmasp came of age, he vowed to reduce the power of the Qizibash and he did this by introducing a new stratum of society. His policy was to annex the Caucasus, and in the process seize Circassian, Georgian and Armenian slaves. Analogous to the Ottoman Janissary system, Tahmasp then placed the Caucasian slaves into the military, administration and court. Sometimes referred to as the *Ghilman* (slave-soldier), or the 'Third Force', the Caucasians rose up in the ranks and gradually replaced the Qizilbash.

Throughout the Safavid period, relations with the Ottoman Empire overshadowed all else. This resulted in several attempts to form a Habsburg-Safavid alliance against the Ottomans, the common enemy. Negotiations started during the reign of Ismail I, and between 1516 and 1523, a Maronite friar from Syria, named Petrus de Monte Libano, travelled between the European and Persian courts carrying proposals for joint military action against the Ottomans. However, due to the distances and time involved in carrying the diplomatic messages, the proposal failed to materialise. During the same period, an Ottoman-French alliance was formed against the Habsburgs.

In 1529, when the Ottoman Sultan Sulieman the Magnificent reached the walls of Vienna, Charles V, the Habsburg Holy Roman Emperor, fearing Ottoman incursions deeper into Europe, resurrected negotiations with the Safavids. Although Shah Tahmasp was willing to take joint action against the Ottomans, he was forced to redirect his forces to the East, in order to deal with an Uzbek insurrection. Despite this, negotiations between the Habsburgs and Safavids continued sporadically until about 1615.

While relations with the Sunni Ottomans were difficult, those with the Sunni Mughals of India were generally good, despite the fact that the Safavids were Shi'a. The founder of the Mughal Empire, Babur, was a descendent of Timur. He was born in Fergana, present day Uzbekistan, and at various times was ruler of Kabul and Samarkand. In 1526, he crossed the River Indus and after defeating Ibrahim Lodi, the Afghan ruler of Delhi, at the Battle of Panipat, he established the Mughal Empire with its capital in Delhi.

Babur was succeeded as Mughal Emperor in 1530 by his son Humayun, but he was ousted ten years later by Sher Shah Suri, an ethnic Pashtun. Humayun was forced into exile with his young wife, who was then bearing Akbar, the third Mughal Emperor, later known as 'Akbar the Great'. Humayan spent fifteen in exile at the Safavid court of Shah Tahmasp. He returned to Dellhi in 1555 and with military aid provided by the Safavids he was able to reclaim his empire. Humayan also took with him

Persian artisans, architects, artists and scholars, all of whom would contribute to the unique Mughal architectural style known as Indo-Islamic. Humayan's Tomb and the Taj Mahal are just two examples that have survived to this day.

Shah Abbas the Great: 1588-1629

While Tahmasp was the longest-reigning Shah of the Safavids, Abbas I was perhaps the strongest ruler. A key element of Abbas's rule was his expansion and consolidation of the Ghilman system that had earlier been introduced by Shah Tahmasp. Consequently, by the end of the 16th Century, the Iranian Qizalbash were virtually eclipsed by the Ghilman. Abbas also reformed the Safavid military.

With the infrastructure of the Empire strengthened through the Ghilman, and the military improved through reform, Abbas was able to retake territory in the Caucasus and Mesopotamia that had previously been lost to the Ottomans. With the help of the English, he also regained coastal ports along the Persian Gulf that had been seized by the Portuguese, and he took back areas of today's Pakistan and Afghanistan that had been annexed by the Mughals.

While Abbas was known to treat minority Sunni Muslims harshly, his attitude towards Armenian Christians was generally more tolerant. In 1604, when the Safavids conducted a scorched-earth policy along the border with the Ottoman Empire, hundreds of thousands of Armenian Christians were displaced. They were then forced to march to Abbas's new city of Isfahan, where he re-settled those who survived the march in their own quarter, known as New Julfa. He built them a cathedral and many Armenians worked on the embellishment of his new city.

At the time, Abbas was keen to establish good relations with Christian states in Europe as potential allies against the Ottomans. Consequently, his apparent tolerant policy towards the Armenians was possibly motivated by pragmatism rather than a genuine wish for inter-religious harmony. This did not work in the case of the Georgian Christians however, many of whom he forced to convert to Islam, sometimes under torture.

140

In around 1614, Shah Abbas invaded the Kingdom of Kakheti, which was the eastern part of today's Georgia. His intention was to bring the Kingdom firmly under Safavid rule. When the Kakhetians resisted, the Safavid response was brutal. Up to 70,000 peasants were massacred and over a hundred thousand forcibly exiled to Iran, leaving the region economically weak and virtually depopulated. In 1659, Shah Abbas II attempted to settle Qizalbash Turkic tribes in the region. This led to a mass uprising among the Kakhetians which was just one element that contributed to the fall of the Safavids.

Decline of the Safavids

Throughout the period of Safavid rule, the Ottomans sought to annex Safavid territory in the northwest. In order to counter-act this, numerous attempts were made to form an alliance with the Habsburg rulers of the Holy Roman Empire, and also with the Papacy. But none resulted in decisive action, partly due to disagreements over the Straits of Hormuz. Furthermore, the Papacy's proposal that the Armenians should convert to Catholicism as a condition of any alliance, was unacceptable to the Safavids.

There were also sporadic invasions and uprisings by the Uzbek Khanates in the northeast. In the east, the Mughal Empire, with its capital in Delhi, encroached upon Safavid territory in Afghanistan, such as Kabul and Kandahar. But by the middle of the 17th Century, there was a new threat; the Tsardom of Russia, whose expansionist policies included the conquest of the Caucasus and Siberia. This brought the Russians dangerously close to Safavid territory in Central Asia.

The Safavids were also undermined by the growing maritime power of the Dutch, and later English, East India Companies. As vital sea-ports in the Persian Gulf fell to the European powers, the Safavids lost access to markets in Arabia, East Africa and India. In order to compensate, the Persians strengthened their overland trade routes and it was during this time that the Persian rug industry expanded into Europe.

Shah Abbas died of natural causes in 1629. Of his five sons, three survived to adulthood. But like many autocratic rulers of the time, the Shah had been obsessed with the fear of assassination. On different occasions, he suspected his sons of plotting against him. In each case Shah Abbas had them blinded, imprisoned or murdered. With no surviving son to succeed him, the throne was passed to his 18-year-old grandson who took the name Shah Safi. Apart from being cruel, he proved to be the first of a succession of weak rulers until the final demise of the Empire.

The Safavid Empire survived for another hundred years, albeit in a weakened position. In March 1736, the Empire was disestablished when Nader Shah Afshar was crowned Shah of Iran.

Nader Shah: 1736-1747

Nader Shah was born in Khorasan, in the north-eastern part of the Iranian Empire. He belonged to a clan of the Afshars, who were semi-nomadic Turkic pastoralists. When he lost his father at the age of 13, he was forced to sell firewood in order to survive. According to tradition, when he was about 17, he and his mother were carried off into slavery by an Uzbek tribe. While his mother died in captivity, details of Nader's escape are unclear. In later years, while on campaign, he would recount his early years to his troops, reminding them that anyone was capable of rising from humble origins through the ranks, as he had done.

For many years, the Afshars had fought for the Safavids and it was in this context that Nader was first recognised for his military skills. When the Safavid Shah, Tahmasp II, made him a general, Nader excelled himself by ousting those foreign powers that had occupied Safavid territory. Eventually he became so powerful that, with the support of the military and the people, he was able to challenge Tahmasp for the throne. In March 1736, he was crowned Shahanshah of Persia.

Apart from being one of the greatest military tacticians of all time, Nader was also a pragmatist. An example of this would be his attitude towards religion. While not known to be particularly religious himself, he was aware of the way that religion had affected the relationship between the Ottomans, who were Sunni, and the Safavids, who were Shi'a. In order to overcome this problem, Nader Shah proposed a new form of Shi'ism, known as Ja'fari, named after the sixth Shi'a Imam, Ja'far al-Sadiq. One of the key elements of this new religion was to ban the Shi'a tradition of cursing the first three Caliphs, who were revered by the Sunni, but rejected by the Shi'a.

Nader hoped that this change in policy would make Ja'fari more palatable to the Sunni Ottomans and consequently improve relations between the two powers, as well as help smooth tensions within his own army between the Sunni and Shi'a. An outward expression of the new Ja'fari religion was the so-called *kolah-e Naderi,* which was a hat with four peaks, representing all four of the first Caliphs, as revered by the Sunni. His hopes that Ja'fari would be recognised as one of the officially recognised *mahdabs* (school of Islamic thought) did not materialise. However, he did succeed in getting permission from the Ottomans for his Shi'a subjects to go on pilgrimage to Mecca, which was in Ottoman territory. It was also agreed that Shi'a subjects of the Ottoman Empire would be given access to Shi'a shrines in Iraq.

Invasion of India: 1738

For many decades, the Mughals and Safavids had competed for territory in the region of modern Afghanistan, which was officially under the vassalage of the Persians. In 1738, while Nader Shah was attempting to quell an insurgency in the region, many Afghans sought refuge with the Mughals in India. When the Mughals refused to hand the Afghans over to the Persians, Nader Shah used this as an excuse to invade India.

In February 1739, the Persians and Mughals confronted each other at the Battle of Karnal, in the region of today's Punjab. Although the Persians were outnumbered by three to one, Nader Shah won a decisive victory over the Mughals in just three hours. The Mughal Emperor, Muhammad Shah, was forced to capitulate. He was then marched to Delhi where he witnessed the massacre of thousands of his citizens and the sack of the city. Although the Mughals were militarily weak, due to the rise of the Sikhs and Marathas, they were still extremely wealthy. Nader Shah looted the entire treasury. His most prized gains included the Peacock Throne, that had been commissioned by the Mughal Emperor Shah Jahan, and the famous Koh-i-Noor diamond, which is now part of the British Crown Jewels.

It is said that Nader needed 700 elephants, 4,00 camels and 12,000 horses to carry his loot back to Persia. With this amount of treasure, he was able to relieve his people of taxation for three years and he still had sufficient money for his campaigns against the Ottomans.

Fall of Nader Shah: 1747

As so often happens with powerful rulers, Nader Shah became increasingly paranoid and obsessed with the fear of assassination. Consequently, his acts of cruelty, especially against those he suspected, grew. Towers of the skulls of those who opposed him, became common-place, almost on a par with those of Timur. By the mid 1740s, because he had spent most of the money seized from the Mughals, he increased taxation.

In June, 1747, Nader Shah met his death in the town of Quchan, Khorasan, at the hands of assassins. Afshars and Qajars were among the fifteen assailants but despite their number, the Shah was able to kill two of them before he died.

In recognition of his great military skills, Nader Shah has been variously referred to as the Napoleon of Persia, the Sword of Persia, or the Second Alexander. Throughout his life he idolised Genghis Khan and Timur. After his death, his empire fell into anarchy and chaos. During a five-year period of civil war, many states declared independence, including the Uzbek Khanates of Bukhara and Khiva and the Caucasian states of Azerbaijan, Armenia and Dagestan. At around the same time, Bahrain in the Persian Gulf, was lost to the Arabian House of Khalifa. But perhaps the most crucial loss of Nader Shah's Afsharid Dynasty was in the East, where Ahmad Shah Durrani established modern Afghanistan.

Conclusion

Timur, known in the West as Tamerlane, came to power in the context of the fall of the Mongol Empire. Furthermore, his defeat of the Golden Horde in 1395, contributed to the end of Mongol rule in Russia and also led to a growing awareness in Western Europe of a new threat from the East.

Timur's greatest ambition had been to reunite the original states of the Mongol Empire that had been conquered by Genghis Khan. To this end, he idolised the Great Khan. Although from a different clan to Genghis, Timur, who was Turkic-Mongol, claimed to be his descendent, both through a common ancestry and by marriage. However, unlike Genghis, who lived a nomadic life and practised Tengrism, Timur unashamedly conquered by the 'Sword of Islam' and far from being a nomad, he built great cities, such as Samarkand and Bukhara, albeit at the cost of some 70 million lives.

The long-term consequences of Timur's campaigns were significant. His capture of Delhi in 1398, served as self-justification for Babur, his direct descendent, to conquer the city in 1526, prior to founding the Mughal Empire. And when Timur clashed with the Ottomans in 1402 at the Battle of Ankara, this marked the beginning of around 300 years' tension between the Ottomans and Persians.

Apart from territorial expansion, the Timurid period was also known for its significant cultural achievement, often being referred to as the Timurid Renaissance. It was a time that witnessed a synthesis of Mughal, Persian, Chinese and Seljuk influences, the best example being the Islamic-Persian architecture of the Mughals. This was also the period when the Timurids were making advances in the manufacture of firearms, skills that would be inherited by the Ottomans and Mughals.

The Timurid Empire could be seen as a transition period between the successor states of the 'nomadic' Mongol Empire, and the more centralised 'modern' states, typified by the 'Gunpowder Empires', e.g. the Ottomans, Safavids and Mughals.

When Timur died in 1450, his Empire was divided among his sons. This resulted in the decline of the Timurid Dynasty, apart from in India where the dynasty continued as the Mughal Empire until 1857. The Central Asian states in Transoxiana broke up into the independent Khanates of Bukhara and Khiva, both of which would eventually become pawns in the struggle between the Russians and British for dominance in the region.

The greatest part of the Timurid Empire fell to the Safavid Dynasty. The founding of the Safavid Empire by Ismail I in 1502, marked a watershed in Iranian history in a number of ways. First, after centuries of foreign rule, it was to be the first native Iranian dynasty since the Sassanids (224-651). Second, the Safavids introduced Shi'ism as the official state religion, and third, the founding of the Empire can be seen as marking the beginning of modern Iran.

When Shah Ismail I founded the dynasty in 1501, he was very much influenced by Sufism, particularly as practised by the military/religious order of the Qizilbash. Consequently, the Qizilbash played a key role not only in the Safavid army, but they also gained senior posts in the administration. By the time that Shah Tahmasp came to the throne in 1524, he believed that the Qizilbash had become too powerful. To counteract this, he ordered the annexation of parts of the Caucasus with the specific intention of seizing Circassians, Georgians and Armenians for resettlement in Iran. In this way, he created a new level of society that would eventually overshadow the Qizilbash. It was a policy that was continued and even strengthened under Shah Abbas I.

Throughout the period of Safavid rule, relations with the Ottomans remained contentious. As a result, although there were ongoing negotiations with the Habsburgs, aimed at forming a military alliance, nothing materialised.

Shah Abbas the Great was the last strong ruler of the Safavids. When he died in 1629, the Empire went into a steady decline. This was exacerbated by the loss of territory to the Ottomans, the Mughals and the growing power of the Russians. At the same time, the presence of the Dutch and English maritime powers in the Persian Gulf and Indian Ocean, cut off valuable overseas trade.

When Nader Shah came to the throne in 1736, he was able to reclaim some of the lost territory. His reign is also marked by two events. First, his attempt to introduce an innovative form of Shi'ism called Ja'fari, in the hope of improving relations with the Sunni Ottomans, and second, his brutal sack of Delhi.

Nader Shah was the last great Central Asian conqueror. When he died in 1747, the region fell into anarchy and became vulnerable to its predatory neighbours. It was a pattern that had been repeated numerous times in the past. Only a strong ruler, such as Timur, Abbas the Great or Nader Shah was able to hold an empire together. At times of weakness, especially as a Shi'a state, it was frequently attacked by its Sunni neighbours, the Ottomans and Mughals.

By the middle of the 18th Century, the threat to Central Asia came primarily from the Russians and the British, as each competed for dominance in a conflict that became known as the 'Great Game'.

*****

CHAPTER TEN
The Great Game: 1830-1895

The term, 'the Great Game', *Le grand jeu,* in French, can be traced back at least as far as the late 16th Century when it was associated with games of risk, such as cards and dice and those involving deception. It was first coined, in reference to the rivalry between Britain and Russia, in July 1840, by Captain Arthur Conolly. He was an Intelligence Officer with the British East India Company and was writing at the time to Major Henry Rawlinson, a British agent stationed at Kandahar. Conolly suggested to Rawlinson that he had 'a great game and noble game' ahead of him in the advancement of Afghanistan. Rudyard Kipling's popular novel *Kim,* also brought the attention of the British people to the 19th Century rivalry between Britain and Russia. However, the term did not come into general usage until after the Second World War, and there is no general consensus over the exact date as to when the 'Game' began and when it finished.

Afghanistan was then, as now, strategically important, being at the crossroads between Central Asia, Russia, and the Indian subcontinent. During the 19th Century, the country was pivotal in the conflict between Russia and Britain, as each competed for influence in the region.

As early as 1717, Peter the Great had sent a delegation to the Khanate of Khiva offering Russian protection in exchange for trading rights to the rich mineral resources of the Oxus delta that he desperately needed to pay for his European wars. The Khan rejected the offer and massacred most of the Russian delegation. However, as part of Russia's eastwards expansion, Cossacks continued to make inroads into Central Asia. Russia also believed that the British presence in the region posed a direct threat to her own trade ambitions. Britain, on the other hand, suspected that Russia's ultimate aim was to gain access to India, Britain's 'Jewel in the Imperial Crown'.

At the beginning of the 19th Century, the French also had territorial ambitions in British India. Napoleon's initial plan had been to launch an invasion from Egypt, but his navy was virtually destroyed in 1798 by Horatio Nelson at the Battle of the Nile. Consequently, he was forced to consider an overland route and he discussed a joint Russian/French invasion with Emperor Paul I of Russia. Nothing materialised, however. First, because Russo/French relations deteriorated under Paul's successor, Alexander I, and second, the French threat declined following Napoleon's defeat at the Battle of Borodino in 1812.

The defence of India was hotly debated in the British Parliament. Opinion was divided between the Russophobes, who called for an aggressive 'Forward Policy', and those who recommended a 'Backward', or inactive policy. Those who recommended the 'Forward Policy, believed that the best strategy was to gain the loyalty of the Central Asian Khanates ahead of the Russians. The strategy was to make Afghanistan a protectorate and use the Ottoman and Persian Empires, as well as the Khanates of Khiva and Bukhara, as buffer states against Russia. The more cautious advocates of an inactive policy, doubted the seriousness of the Russian threat, largely on the grounds that any invading army from the north would face the challenge of an unknown and inhospitable terrain that was inhabited by dangerous warlike tribes.

The early explorers

Britain and France were sea powers and therefore, for them, control of sea the routes had been paramount for centuries. But with the onset of the Great Game, the focus in the region changed to overland routes from Persia and Russia to India. However, knowledge of the Central Asian terrain was extremely limited, and in some cases based on little more than the campaigns of Alexander the Great centuries earlier. (See Chapter 3) Consequently, the British employed Indian hill men, disguised as Hindu or Muslim holy men, as guides and often as spies, while the Russians used Mongol tribesmen disguised as Buddhist monks. But the primary task of mapping the region and intelligence gathering on both sides was undertaken by Europeans.

In 1810, Lieutenant Henry Pottinger and Captain Charles Christie, both officers with the British East India Company, were commissioned to map the route from Nushki in Pakistan to Isfahan in Central Iran. The purpose was to assess the viability of a Russian or French overland invasion of India.

Disguised as Muslim horse dealers, the two men took different routes. Pottinger travelled 900 miles westwards across the Central Asian deserts. During the difficult journey, he described his throat as being *'so parched and dry that you respire with difficulty, to dread moving your tongue in your mouth from the apprehensions of suffocating...'*. (Peter Hopkirk, *The Great Game, On Secret Service in High Asia*)

Christie first travelled north to Herat, a city renowned for its horses. He then journeyed on to Isfahan, where the two men were reunited on the 10th June 1810. Their journeys had taken over three months. Christie had ridden 2,250 miles and Pottinger over 2,400 miles. Throughout their travels, the two men gathered intelligence concerning the tribes, their leaders and numbers of fighting men, as well as the location of wells, rivers, crops and vegetation, all information that would prove invaluable in the future.

Ten years later, in 1820, William Moorcroft led an expedition to Bukhara. Trained as a vet, Moorcroft first travelled to India in 1808, to take up the position of Superintendent of the Stud for the East India Company. Ostensibly, the purpose of the journey to Bukhara was to buy the famous pale golden Turkoman horses, known for their speed and stamina, and much talked about in the bazaars of Northern India. Although his expedition was financed by the East India Company, Moorcroft had no official status and could not rely on British help if he got into difficulties.

Moorcroft departed from India on the 16th March 1820. He was accompanied by George Trebeck, a young Englishman and George Guthrie, an Anglo-Indian. Their caravan totalled 300 persons, including a number of Gurkhas as well as some of the finest British goods which Moorcroft hoped to trade with the Khanates. As a staunch Russophobe, Moorcroft was a firm believer in the Forward Policy and he thought that Britain should be ahead of the Russians in establishing good relations, initially through trade, with the Khanates.

Because of a civil war raging in the area, the caravan was forced to by-pass Afghanistan, which would have been the most direct route to Bukhara. The safest route was via Leh, the capital of Ladakh, in Chinese Turkestan. It was while in Leh that Moorcroft discovered that the Russians were ahead of the game. A Russian by the name of Meghti Rafailov, had been trading in Chinese Turkestan for some time and Russian goods were to be found in the bazaars. But Tsar Alexander I had commissioned Rafailov to travel even further South into the Punjab and open diplomatic negotiations with the Sikh ruler, Ranjit Singh, who at the time was on friendly terms with the British.

Moorcroft's warnings about Russia's intentions were ignored by the officials of the East India Company and so he decided to take things into his own hands by negotiating a commercial treaty with the ruler of Ladakh in exchange for British protection. Unfortunately, Ladakh was within Ranjit Singh's sphere of influence. Fearful of upsetting the Sikhs, the British repudiated the treaty and suspended Moorcroft's salary.

Despite his problems, Moorcroft and his party continued on their journey, arriving in Kashmir in 1822 and Kabul in June 1824. While in Kabul, they became the first Europeans to visit the famous Buddhas of Bamiyan that were unfortunately destroyed by the Taliban in 2001.

In February 1825, Moorcroft reached Bukhara. He did not find the famed horses, and to his disappointment, he discovered that the Russians had reached Bukhara four years previously. Moorcroft and his two companions died of fever six months later while on their return journey to India. He had been travelling for almost six years, during which time he wrote almost 10,000 pages of manuscript which were later obtained by the Asiatic Society. The papers were eventually published as *Travels in the Himalayan Provinces of Hindustan and the Punjab, in Ladakh and Kashnair, in Peshawur, Kabul, Kunduz and Bokhara, from 1819 to 1825.*

Other intrepid explorers followed. In 1829, Lieutenant Arthur Connolly of the British East India Company, travelled from St Petersburg to India via Astrabad in northern Iran, where he was arrested on suspicion of being a Russian spy. He then marched with the Afghan army as far as Herat and finally reached British India in January 1831. His travels were published in 1834 as *A Journey to the North of India through Russia, Persia and Afghanistan.*

Captain Sir Alexander Burnes' book, *Travels to Bukhara,* became an overnight best seller in the same year. Burnes, who was a first-cousin of the poet Robert Burns, joined the East India Company at the age of 16 and became proficient in Persian and Urdu. By 1831, the British Government had begun to take the Russian threat seriously and so Burnes was commissioned to make a survey of the route from Kabul to Bukhara, as well as collect intelligence on Afghan politics. His book tells the story of how he travelled in disguise, first sailing up the Indus River and then on to Lahore, where he presented gifts from King William IV to the Sikh Ruler, Maharaja Ranjit Singh.

Founding of Afghanistan: 1747

Ahmad Shah Durrani, an ethnic Pashtun of the Sadozai tribe, is credited with founding the modern state of Afghanistan. Ahmad was born in Herat in 1722. His father was the Governor of Herat at a time when the region came under the rule of Nader, Shah of Iran. (see Chapter Nine) When the Shah was assassinated in 1747, the Afghan tribes chose Ahmad as their leader, marking the beginning of an Afghan entity that was independent of either the Persians or the Mughals. It is said that when Nadir Shah was assassinated, Ahmad removed the *Koh-i-Noor* diamond from the arm-band of the dead man, thus the famous gem passed from the Persians to the Afghans.

By gaining the loyalty of the tribes, Ahmad was able to unite a region that straddled today's Afghanistan, Pakistan, north-eastern Iran and Turkmenistan. He was also able to wrest parts of north-west India from the Mughals. The Mughals had been in steady decline since the death of Emperor Aurangzeb in 1707 and had lost territory to both the British East India Company and the powerful Hindu Maratha Empire. The Afghan incursion into north-west India brought it into conflict with the Marathas and a fierce battle took place between the two powers at the Third

Battle of Panipat in 1761. The result was a decisive victory for the Afghans and an awakening for the British in India to the fact that the Afghans posed a serious threat on their western border.

Ahmad Shah Durrani died on the 16th October, 1772 in Kandahar. As the founder of modern Afghanistan, he is often referred to as 'Ahmad Shah the Father'. Mountstuart Elphinstone, the Scottish statesman and historian, who spent time with the East India Company, wrote that *'His military courage and activity are spoken of with admiration, both by his own subjects and the nations with whom he was engaged, either in wars or alliances. He seems to have been naturally disposed to mildness and clemency'*.

SIGNIFICANT AFGHAN RULERS		
Ahmad Shah	Durrani	1747-1772
Timur Shah	Durrani	1772-1793
Zaman Shah	Durrani	1793-1801
Shah Shuja	Durrani	1803-1809 1839-1842
Dost Muhammad	Barakzai	1823-1839 1845-1863
Sher Ali Khan	Barakzai	1863-1865 1868-1879
Abdur Rahman Khan	Barakzai	1880-1901

Timur Shah Durrani, the eldest son of Ahmad, succeeded his father as Shah of the Durrani Empire and married the daughter of the Mughal Emperor Alamgir II. Consequently, he was influenced by Mughal/Persian culture and was never very popular with the Afghan tribes. In an attempt to remove himself from the quarrelsome Pashtun clans, he moved the capital from Kandahar to Kabul and made Peshawar his winter capital. Timur died in 1793 and left 24 sons. He was succeeded by his fifth son,

Zaman Shah Durrani. However, two other sons, Mahmud Shah and Shah Shujah, also competed for the throne, a situation that eventually led to civil war.

Zaman acquired the throne in 1793 with the help of Payindah Khan, leader of the Barakzai tribe. A few years later, when the two men had an argument, Zaman reacted by executing not only Payinday Khan, but many of his tribal elders. By so doing, he not only set in motion a blood feud between the Sadozai and the Barakzai, the two most powerful of the Afghan tribes, but he also undid the balance of power between the tribes that Ahmad Shah had worked so hard to maintain.

In 1800, Zaman was captured, imprisoned and blinded on the instigation of his half-brother Mahmud Shah, who then held the throne until 1803. After spending some years imprisoned in Kabul, Zaman was then given refuge, first in Lahore by the Sikh leader Ranjit Singh and then by the British at the frontier city of Ludhiana, where he lived in relative comfort with a pension paid for by the East India Company.

In July, 1803, Shah Shujah Durrani ascended the throne as King of Afghanistan. One of his first tasks was to attempt to end the blood feud with the Barakzai tribe through a marriage alliance. However, he made a far more significant alliance with the British in 1809. As part of Britain's strategy aimed at averting a French or Russian invasion, Mountstuart Elphinstone was commissioned to lead the first ever delegation to Afghanistan. His task was to persuade Shah Shujah to agree to block any foreign power from passing through Afghan territory en route for India. In exchange, the Shah was promised British protection from any foreign aggression against his territories at a time when the Persians, the Russians and the Sikhs all posed a potential threat to Afghanistan.

The alliance made in 1809 would be the first of many that ultimately undermined Afghan sovereignty. However, this first alliance proved to be ineffectual because almost immediately, Shah Shujah was ousted by his brother Mahmud Shah Durrani. After imprisonment in Kashmir, Shah Shujah then fell into the hands of the Sikhs and was imprisoned in Lahore. While in confinement, he was forced to give up the Koh-i-Noor diamond to Ranjit Singh. Thus, the valuable gem passed from the Afghans to the Sikhs.

In 1818, Shah Shujah managed to escape to British India where he lived a life of luxury in Ludhiana. For the next twenty years, he and his court in exile was funded by the East India Company. The British believed that Shujah could prove useful in the future. If he were reinstated as King of Afghanistan, he could be a valuable ally and supportive of British policy in the region. The fact that Shah Shujah spoke openly of his plans to retake his throne, reinforced British aspirations.

First Anglo-Afghan War: 1839-1842

During the years that Shah Shuja was in exile in India, the Sodozai (Durrani) dynasty fractured, while the Barakzai tribe grew in power. A watershed moment came when Dost Mohammad, the eleventh son of Sardar Payendah Khan, chief of the Barakzai tribe, claimed the title of Emir of Afghanistan in 1826.

Apart from having a personal grievance against the Durranis, who had executed his father in 1799, Dost Mohammad had also made enemies of the Sikhs, who had seized Peshawar, Afghanistan's second capital city. In the hope of retaking Peshawar, Dost Mohammad approached the British, proposing joint Afghan/British military action to retake the city. However, although the British were keen to remain on friendly terms with the Afghans, they felt that this could not be at the expense of upsetting the Sikhs, with their formidable French-trained military, the *Dal Khalsa*. This was a dilemma that frequently confronted the British.

Having been rejected by the British, it was not surprising therefore, that the Afghans would turn to the Russians. British fears of Russia's involvement were confirmed in December 1837 by Alexander Burnes. He happened to be present in Kabul, working as a British agent at the same time as the Russian envoy,

Yan Vitkevitch. When Lord Auckland, Governor-General of India, heard of this, in January 1838, he wrote to the Afghan ruler:

"You must desist from all correspondence with Russia. You must never receive Agents from them, or have aught to do with them without our sanction. You must dismiss Captain Viktevitch with courtesy; you must surrender all claims to Peshawar". (Macintyre Ben, *The Man Who Would Be King*, New York: Farrar, Straus, Giroux)

Fearing that Dost Mohammad would ally with the Russians, in November 1838, Lord Auckland ordered an invasion of Afghanistan with the aim of removing him from the throne and installing the 'rightful' claimant, Shah Shujah of the Durrani dynasty who was then living in India at the expense of the British. The fact that Shah Shujah had been deposed around thirty years previously, that he was hardly known by the majority of Afghans and was extremely unpopular among those who did remember him, was seen to be irrelevant.

In December 1838, a joint Sikh/British army of 21,000 troops, plus some 38,000 camp followers, set off from the Punjab. 30,000 camels were needed to carry personal effects. One regiment took a pack of foxes for hunting and up to 40 servants accompanied each officer. The size and make-up of the train would indicate that this was not simply a small army escorting the return of a rightful King, but that the British intended to remain in Afghanistan for some length of time.

By the end of April 1839, British troops had taken Kandahar unopposed and in July they captured the fortress of Ghazni. In the face of the British advance, Dost Mohammad's fighters began to desert and he fled with a few loyal supporters first to Bukhara, and he later lived in exile in India. By August, Shah Shujah had been reinstated as King of Afghanistan.

The British claimed that their presence in Kabul was necessary in order to ensure a smooth transition of rule from Dost Mohammad to Shah Shuja. They initially set up their headquarters in the Bala Hissar fortress and later moved to a cantonment which was away from the general population of the city. However, when foreign wives and children began to arrive, the Afghans suspected the British motive to be one of 'occupation'.

Resentment towards the British presence grew when it became evident that foreign troops were having sexual relations with Afghan women. In such a conservative Islamic society, where honour killings were commonplace, conflict was inevitable. Even Alexander Burnes, who had been on extremely good relations with the Afghans, angered the people with his behaviour towards local women.

It was an incident in the home of Burnes, on the evening of the 1st November 1841, that proved to be the spark that lit the fire of rebellion. When it was discovered that he had not only given refuge to a runaway slave girl, but that he had slept with her, the Council of Pashtun Chiefs felt justified in declaring a *Jihad* against the British. The following morning, the people went on the rampage, looting shops and seeking revenge. In the havoc, Burnes was hacked to death.

After weeks of violent riots that resulted in many deaths on all sides, the Afghans agreed to the safe withdrawal of the British garrison. On the 6th January 1842, some 4,500 military and 12,000 camp followers, including British, Indian and a few Afghan women, began a long and hazardous journey, in the middle of winter, towards Jalalabad. Florentia Sale, (Lady Sale, wife of Colonel Robert Sale, describes the 80-mile struggle, through the snow-covered mountain passes, in her book, *Lady Sale's Afghanistan: an Indomitable Victorian Lady's Account of the Retreat from Kabul During the First Afghan War.*

Despite promises of safe passage, the convoy was attacked by Ghilzai tribesmen as it passed through the five-mile narrow gorge known as the Koord-Kabul Pass in the Hindu Kush. Of those who had not already frozen to death, most of the women and children were taken captive. The men were slaughtered in cold blood. Of the six soldiers who managed to escape on horseback, only one, Dr William Brydon, reached Jalalabad.

In April 1842, the British launched a punitive attack and retook Kabul. The city's nobles were executed by hanging and the central bazaar was burned to the ground. Shah Shujah, who had been hiding in the Bala Hissar fortress, was assassinated by his own people. By September, most of the women and children were released from captivity, but a small number of women stayed behind as wives of local Afghans. Finally, the new Governor General, Lord Ellenborough, ordered the withdrawal of all British troops from Afghanistan and Dost Mohammad Khan returned from exile to take up his throne.

According to Martin Ewens, (*Afghanistan: A short History of its People and Politics*), Dost Mohammad is said to have remarked to the British:

I have been struck by the magnitude of your resources, your ships, your arsenals, but what I cannot understand is why the rulers of so vast and flourishing an empire should have gone across the Indus to deprive me of my poor and barren country.

Second Anglo-Afghan War: 1878-1880

By 1878, the Emir of Afghanistan was Sher Ali Khan, son of Dost Mohammad. The situation in India had also changed. Following the Indian Uprising in 1857, rule in British India had been transferred from the East India Company to a Viceroy and Governor General who was directly responsible to the British Crown in London. At the same time, Russia's year-long war with the Ottomans had ended with the signing of the Treaty of Berlin. Consequently, Russia now had sufficient resources to turn her attention once again to Central Asia.

Despite the above changes, Iran and Afghanistan continued to compete for control over the strategically important city of Herat. But more significantly, tensions between Russia and Britain, fuelled by the press on both sides of the conflict, remained. Eventually, both powers concluded that an aggressive policy, rather than diplomacy, was more likely to gain the loyalty of the Central Asian Khanates. As Britain strengthened her hold over Afghanistan and the Sikh territory of the Punjab, Russia either annexed, or brought into her sphere of influence, Tashkent (1865), Samarkand (1868) and Khiva (1873).

Although Afghan policy was to remain neutral in the conflict between Russia and Britain, in July 1878, Russia sent a diplomatic mission to meet with Sher Ali Khan. The envoy was neither invited nor welcome. When the British heard of the Russian presence in Kabul, they insisted that a British mission should also be received by the Emir. Despite the fact that the Emir refused Britain's request, the Viceroy of India, ordered that a diplomatic mission to Kabul go ahead. However, when the envoys reached the eastern entrance to the Khyber Pass in September 1878, it was turned back by Ali Khan's men. It was an act that sparked the beginning of the Second Anglo-Afghan War.

In November 1878, a British force of some 50,000 men, mostly Indians, invaded Afghanistan. The first battle took place on the 21st November, at the Ali Masjid Fortress, at the western end of the Khyber Pass. Despite the fact that the British forces were in unfamiliar territory and wearing unsuitable uniforms, their superior munitions won them a resounding victory. Following a further British victory at the Battle of Peiwar Kotal, which is located in today's Pakistan, Kabul was left virtually undefended.

Faced with total defeat, Sher Ali Khan appealed to the Russians for help. Not wishing to antagonise the British, the Russians advised the Emir to seek terms of surrender. Ali Khan died three months later in the northern Afghan city of Mazar-i-Sharif. It was therefore left to his son, Mohammad Yaqub Khan, to agree peace terms with the British.

Treaty of Gandamak

On the 26th May 1879, the new Emir signed the Treaty of Gandamak, marking the end of hostilities. Under the terms of the Treaty, Afghanistan ceded territory along her eastern border with British India, including the Khyber Pass, to the British. While the Afghans officially retained sovereignty over the rest of the country, according to the Treaty, they lost control of their foreign policy:

His Highness the Amir will enter into no engagements with Foreign States, and will not take up arms against any Foreign State, except with the concurrence of the British Government. On these conditions the British Government will support the Amir against any foreign aggression with money, arms, or troops, to be employed in whatsoever manner the British Government may judge best for this purpose. Should British troops at any time enter Afghanistan for the purpose of repelling foreign aggression, they will return to their stations in British territory as soon as the object for which they entered has been accomplished.

This clause regarding foreign relations was particularly humiliating for the independent-minded Pashtun tribes. Further provisions allowed for a British mission to be set up in Kabul, increased trade opportunities and the installation of a telegraph line between Kabul and British India.

On the 24th July 1879, a British Mission, led by Pierre Cavagnari, arrived to take up residence in Kabul. Cavagnari was born in Palma. He became a naturalised British citizen and held several important posts with the East India Company. After being a signatory to the Treaty of Gandamak, he was appointed as Britain's Representative in Kabul. But on the 3rd September, less than two months after his arrival in Kabul, Cavagnari and all members of the Mission were murdered by rebellious soldiers. It was an act that led to the second phase of the Second Anglo-Afghan War.

The small Kabul Field Army, the only British force in the country at the time, was quickly reinforced. By the 8th October, British troops managed to retake Kabul, despite the efforts of a force of 10,000 Afghans to defend the city.

Emir Yaqub Khan was suspected of complicity in the murder of Cavagnari and abdicated. The British were then faced with the question of succession between Yaqub's brother, Ayub Khan, who was Governor of Herat, or his cousin, Abdur Rahman Khan. Abdur Rahman Khan was chosen and went on to rule for 21 years. In the meantime, Ayub Khan rose in rebellion and on the 27th July after beating the British at the Battle of Maiwand, he went on to besiege Kandahar. Ayub's victory was short-lived however. The main British forced marched from Kabul and on the 1st September 1879, put down the rebellion at the Battle of Kandahar, so ending the Second Anglo-Afghan War.

Anglo-Russian Agreements

Between the Treaty of Gandamak in 1879 and the Exchange of Notes Between Great Britain and Russia in 1895, there were a number of initiatives and protocols aimed at resolving the conflict between Russia and Britain.

In 1881, as Russian forces came dangerously close to Herat, the two powers set up a joint Anglo-Russian Boundary Commission. Its remit was to define and agree the border between northern Afghanistan and Russia. In September 1885, the Delimitation Protocol Between Great Britain and Russia, was signed in London. This was to be the first of several Protocols aimed at agreeing the border between Russia and Afghanistan.

In November 1893, the British and Afghans agreed the boundary between Afghanistan and British India. Known as the Durand Line, it was named after Mortimer Durand, First Secretary of India. The 800-mile demarcation line cut through the Pashtun and Baloch tribal homelands, leaving ethnic Pashtuns and Balochis on both sides of the border.

Although the Emir of Afghanistan, Abdul Rahman, signed the Agreement, many Afghans have never accepted the boundary, whereas the international community has always recognised the Durand Line as the border, initially between Afghanistan and India, and now between Afghanistan and Pakistan. This is a situation that has contributed to the ongoing instability in Afghanistan. More recently it has proved particularly problematic when tracking down Taliban fighters who are able to cross the border undetected between Afghanistan and Pakistan.

On the 11th March 1895, there was an Exchange of Notes Between Great Britain and Russia that defined the two powers' spheres of influence in the region. This was ratified on the 10th September 1895 with the signing of the Pamir Boundary Commission protocols. This date is generally recognised as marking the end of the Great Game between Russia and Britain.

Conclusion

The 19th Century conflict that became known as the Great Game, occurred within the wider context of the battle between world powers for trade and political influence in Central Asia. The main players were the Russian and British Empires, and to a lesser extent, France and Iran. India, Britain's 'Jewel in the Crown' featured as a prize and the Khans and Emirs of Central Asia became the pawns, while their homelands were the board upon which the big players made their moves.

There is no general consensus as to the exact dates for the beginning or end of the 'Game'. January 1830, when the Governor General of India was asked to establish a trade route between India and Bukhara, is sometimes cited as the start. However, it could also be argued that Napoleon's intentions to join with Russia in an overland invasion of India, at the beginning of the century, marked an early phase of the 'Game'.

An immediate problem that faced all foreign powers was the fact that little was known of the topography of the region, the location of rivers and the accessibility of mountain passes. The same could be said for its inhabitants, the complexity of the tribal system, the number and size of the towns and villages and the strength of their defence forces, both in terms of fortifications and manpower.

The British particularly needed to know how viable it would be for initially the French, and later the Russians, to invade India from an overland route. On the other hand, Russia was concerned that the presence of the British in the region, threatened her expansionist policies in Central Asia.

During the early decades of the 19th Century, both Russia and Britain commissioned map-makers and spies to gather intelligence on the topography and the people. They were fluent in the local languages and usually disguised themselves as traders. Their hazardous journeys often lasted up to six years and risked death from starvation or the cold. Those who did not die from the rigours of the journey, often suffered a gruesome death at the hands of tribesmen. Those who did return brought back valuable information, some of which was later published.

Throughout the period of the Great Game, Afghanistan was ruled by two major Pashtun tribes; the Sadozai, also known as the Durrani, and the Barakzai. Ahmad Shah Durrani, the founder of modern Afghanistan, attempted to unite all the tribes that straddled today's Afghanistan and Pakistan. However, when Zaman Shah Durrani, who came to the throne in 1793, murdered many of the Barakzai leaders, he set in motion a tribal conflict that continued for decades, perhaps even until today.

Britain first became overtly involved in Afghan tribal politics in 1809, when Shah Shuja Durrani allied with the British East India Company. This move was not popular with the majority of the Afghans and when he was overthrown by Dost Mohammad Khan of the Barakzai Khan, Shah Shuja lived in exile in India at the expense of the East India Company. Twenty years later, with the help of the British, he returned to Afghanistan. Britain wanted a 'friendly' ruler on the throne, which meant ousting Dost Mohammad. It was a clear act of 'regime-change' and led indirectly to the First Anglo-Afghan War.

The Treaty of Gandamak (1879), that was signed during the Second Anglo-Afghan War, resulted in further British involvement in Afghanistan. Apart from losing considerable territory along her eastern border, the Afghans forfeited all control of her foreign affairs. Another damaging event was the establishment of the Durand Line that was agreed by the Afghan Emir, Abdur Rahman Khan. The aim was to agree a border between British India (now Pakistan) and Afghanistan, in the hope that this would improve diplomatic and trade relations. But because the line cut through Pashtun and Baloch tribal lands, it has never been officially recognised by many Afghan tribes. Consequently, ethnic Pashtuns and Balochis have always felt free to cross between Afghanistan and Pakistan, a situation that in recent years has enabled the Taliban to thrive.

The conflict along the northern border of Afghanistan between Britain and Russia, was finally settled with the signing of the Pamir Boundary Commission protocols in 1895. While this date marks the end of the Great Game, it did not resolve the conflict between Afghanistan and her more powerful neighbours. In many ways, the British and Russian involvement in the country in the 19th Century, simply laid the ground for an even more turbulent 20th Century.

*****

CHAPTER ELEVEN

Soviet Central Asia

By the beginning of the 20th Century, large swathes of Central Asia, including today's Kazakhstan, Uzbekistan, Turkmenistan, Tajikistan and Kyrgyzstan, had fallen to the Russian Empire. Britain ruled most of India, including today's Pakistan. Afghanistan was a British Protectorate.

Against the growing threat of a German-Ottoman alliance, Russia and Britain agreed to settle their differences over Iran, in order to present a united front against Germany. Under the Anglo-Russian Convention of 1907, Russia acknowledged southern Iran as coming under Britain's sphere of influence, while Britain recognised Russia's influence in the north of the country. At the same time Russia agreed not to interfere in Afghanistan or Tibet.

1916 Central Asian Revolt

In 1916, anti-Russian uprisings spread across Russian Central Asia. There were two main causes for the revolt. First, the mass resettlement of emancipated serfs and peasants from European Russia into Central Asia, sowed discontent among the local population. Beginning with the 1861 Emancipation Reform Act, followed by various land reforms, hundreds of thousands of peasant households had resettled in regions that were often culturally and religiously alien, a situation that inevitably led to social unrest.

The second cause, that actually triggered the revolt, occurred in 1916 when Tsar Nicholas II ordered the conscription of Central Asian men, from the ages of 19 to 43, to work as conscripted labour in front-line positions during World War I.

The protests began in modern-day Tajikistan in the summer of 1916 and quickly spread to Uzbekistan and parts of Kazakhstan and Kyrgyzstan. The rioters targeted Russian settlers and Cossacks who they believed had stolen their lands. Around 3,500 settlers were murdered. Russia's response was brutal, with up to 30,000 Kazakhs and Kyrgyz losing their lives. A further 150,000 died while trying to flee to China. The event is referred to as the

Urkun, or Exodus, and runs deep within Kyrgyz culture. In recent decades, some Central Asian academics have accused Tsarist Russia of genocide, an accusation that is fiercely denied.

Central Asian Soviet Republics

Following the Russian Revolution in 1917 and the fall of the Tsar, colonial Central Asia was initially divided into different Administrative Divisions under Communist rule. The most prominent were the Turkestan Autonomous Soviet Socialist Republic, the Bukharan People's Soviet Republic and the Khorezm People's Soviet Republic. Between 1924 and 1936, these Republics were further divided into five Soviet Socialist Republics that mirror today's Kazakhstan, Uzbekistan, Tajikistan, Turkmenistan and Kyrgystan. In time, these republics developed their own national cultural histories, languages, academic institutions and forms of art.

Protest movements, collectively known as the Basmachi movement, against Tsarist and Soviet Russian rule, came from nationalists, Islamists and other religious minorities, and lasted from 1916 until the outbreak of World War II. Resentment increased as a result of Stalin's Great Purge in 1936-8, when many Chechens, Koreans, and Crimean Tartars were exiled from European Russia to Central Asia. This policy upset the ethnic balance in many cities. By 1980, for example, ethnic Russians made up over 50% of the population of Tashkent.

Stalin's policies also included the persecution of Bukharan Jews, the most isolated Jewish community in the world. Then the forced settlement of Kazakh nomads resulted in a huge loss of livestock. Overall, 1.5 million people died due to starvation and disease. Hundreds of thousands of Islamists and anti-Soviet dissidents found refuge in Afghanistan, British India and Saudi Arabia. To this day, Saudi-based Uzbeks fund the building of mosques in Uzbekistan and ethnic Uzbeks and Tajiks living in Saudi Arabia are known as, Al Bukhari, Al Samarkandi or Al Turkistani, which reflects their city of origin.

During the 1950s and 60s, vast areas of land that straddled Uzbekistan, Tajikistan and Turkmenistan were transformed into cotton plantations in order to feed Soviet industry and provide export material. Unfortunately, these plantations required an extensive irrigation system that contributed to the drying up of the Aral Sea. Other ecological disasters that are a legacy of the Soviet period, include the effects radiation from nuclear testing and an increase in soil salinization.

Soviet-Afghan Relations

Although the Soviet government respected the territorial boundary between Russia and Afghanistan that had been set by the Boundary Commission in 1887, Soviet Russia continued to have considerable influence in the country. During the 1950s, 1960s and 1970s, Afghanistan received large amounts of Soviet military and economic aid. But significantly, Soviet Russia exported Communist ideology to her Central Asian states.

However, the border between Pakistan and Afghanistan, along the Durand Line, continued to cause conflict. As mentioned earlier, when it was created in 1893, the Line split the Pashtun tribes in two, with some Pashtuns living in Afghanistan and others in India (Pakistan after 1847). Mohammed Daoud Khan, who became President of Afghanistan in 1973, promulgated an irredentist policy aimed at reuniting the Pashtun lands. This not only angered Pakistan, but also many Pashtuns living in Pakistan who had no desire to be united with Afghanistan.

At this point, the United States began selling arms to Pakistan as a precaution against possible Afghan aggression across the border. However, when a request from Afghanistan for weapons was rejected by the United States, the Afghans turned to their benefactors, the USSR, for help with military aid.

In 1973, when Mohammed Daoud Khan seized power from his cousin King Zahir, he chose not to take the title of King, or Shah and instead became the President of the Republic of Afghanistan. Although he was a reformist, in that he promoted women's rights etc., his pro-Pashtun policies angered non-Pashtuns and other religious minorities and his anti-monarchist stance was at odds with the majority of conservative Afghans. He also annoyed the Soviets by forging close ties with Western countries. Above all, he became increasingly unpopular with the People's Democratic Party of Afghanistan (PDPA), the most influential Communist party in the country, that had been formed in 1965.

On the 19th April 1978, some 3,00 people, including leaders from all branches of the PDPA, gathered for the funeral of Akbar Khyber, a prominent communist leader who had died under mysterious circumstances. Such a large gathering of Communists alerted Daoud Khan to the strength of the Party and the vulnerability of his own position. Consequently, he ordered the arrest of the main PDPA leaders. This further increased his unpopularity, and on the 28th April 1978, Daoud was overthrown and executed by the Afghan Army. The event is known as the Saur Revolution.

Soviet Invasion of Afghanistan: 1979

Following the overthrow of Daoud Khan, Muhammad Taraki became President and General Secretary of the PDPA. From the outset, the Party was riddled by factionalism. There were two main factions. The Khalq, meaning 'the people', were predominantly Pashtun and favoured a radical form of Marxism, while the Parcham, meaning the 'banner', were primarily the urban elite and believed that a more gradual transition to socialism was best suited to Afghan society. Conflict between the two factions eventually turned violent resulting in the murder of thousands of Parcham by the Khalq.

Despite the internal conflict within the PDPA, the Soviet government continued to support the Party. For example, President Taraki succeeded in securing the deployment of Soviet troops along the Afghan-Soviet border, as well as the services of hundreds of Russian military and civilian special advisers.

The Soviets also encouraged Taraki in his plans for reform. However, since these reforms included women's rights and literacy programmes, they warned Taraki, who belonged to the Khalq faction, to proceed with caution on the grounds that such attempts at modernisation could anger the deeply conservative Afghans.

The PDPA used brutal methods to enforce their reforms, which soon led to social unrest. On the 8th October 1979, President Taraki was assassinated by Hafizullah Amin, who then took over as General Secretary. During the brief period of his rule, which lasted from the 14th September to the 27th December, the Party cracked down on any form of opposition. Up to 30,000 prisoners were executed, including many religious leaders.

Since the spring of 1979, the country had been in a virtual state of civil war, with rebels from the religiously conservative rural population, who became known as the mujahideen, fighting the Afghan government of the PDPA, that was backed by the Soviet Union. However, although the Soviets had supported Afghanistan for decades, and especially since the formation of the PDPA, they watched the unfolding political crisis with great concern, urging the Afghan leadership to resolve their differences. Above all, they were reluctant to intervene in an internal civil war, despite repeated requests from Taraki and Amin for Soviet 'boots on the ground' to help put down the rebels.

The alternative was to be regime change by replacing Amin with their preferred candidate, who was Babrak Kamal of the Parcham faction. When attempts at poisoning Amin failed, Soviet troops stormed the palace in Kabul on the 27th December 1979. In the chaos, Amin was killed and his young son mortally wounded. Initially the Afghans welcomed the Soviets as liberators from a cruel dictatorship. At the time, both Afghanistan and the USSR expected this to be a short-term intervention that had been made at the request of the Afghan government for the benefit of the Afghan people. Neither side predicted this would be the beginning of a brutal and protracted war that would last for ten long years.

The Soviet-Afghan War: 1979-1989

In January 1980, a small number of the Russian elite, including Andrei Sakharov, the famous nuclear physicist, voiced its disapproval of the Soviet invasion. But this was quickly crushed. Others from the military establishment, who still remembered the disastrous Vietnamese war, warned against military intervention in Afghanistan, but were ignored.

With their superior satellite intelligence, the Americans, and less so the British, had been aware of the Soviet presence building up in Afghanistan for several months, but neither the US nor the British knew the true motive behind the invasion. Some speculated that the Russians were ultimately seeking to establish a warm water port in the Persian Gulf, or that the incorporation of Afghanistan into the USSR was part of Soviet imperial policy. By the end of the war, both theories were generally discredited, as analysts from all sides concluded that the Soviets were reacting to the situation on the ground at the time, rather than being proactive as part of an ambitious expansionist programme that they were ill-equipped to fulfil.

The Soviet invasion was widely condemned by the international community. In January 1980, 104 countries supported an American UN resolution condemning the action and there were calls for the boycott of the Olympic Games due to be held in Moscow in the summer of 1980.

Long before the Soviet invasion, the Americans were proposing that the anti-Communist forces should be supported, and in the summer of 1979, President Carter authorised a budget of $500,000 to aid the rebels. According to Rodric Braithwaite, in his publication *Afgantsy: The Russians in Afghanistan, 1979-89,* by 1991, this amount then increased to $9 billion, which was funnelled through Pakistan for distribution to the various mujahideen groups. This was further supplemented by substantial sums from Saudi Arabia and the Gulf States. China also supported the mujahideen, as did Britain by providing the insurgents with arms and military training.

Discussions were also held between the Americans, British and French concerning a joint effort to help the mujahideen and it was suggested by some that Christianity and Islam should unite against the godless Soviet Communists. The American congressman Charlie Wilson argued that the Russians had been responsible for the death of 58,000 Americans during the

Vietnam War and that the US needed to settle the score. The 2007 film, *Charlie Wilson's War,* tells the story of the Congressman, played by Tom Hanks, who campaigned in support of the Afghan rebels. Another factor that influenced America's attitude at the time was the 1979 Iranian Revolution when 52 US diplomats were held hostage for 444 days. A firm handling of the Soviet invasion might therefore go some way towards redressing that humiliation in the eyes of the world and perhaps more importantly, in the opinion of US citizens.

According to the Soviets, the task facing the 40th Army was to enable the warring factions within the PDPA to resolve their differences, to secure the major towns and roads and withdraw once the Afghan government was able to resume its responsibility. The hope was that a stable government would result in law and order, leading to better health and education provision as well as agricultural reform. However, the Soviets would discover, as the British had in the previous century, that most Afghans were fiercely protective of their own way of life and had no desire to have the ways of the foreign infidel imposed upon them.

The main strategy, on both sides in the war, was to disrupt supply lines; the rebel supplies coming across the border from Pakistan and the Soviet supplies from the USSR. In the process, the Soviets carpet-bombed roads and villages and planted thousands of mines along strategic routes. Thousands of civilians, particularly children, were maimed by the mines and the danger of undetonated mines remains to this day

Initially, the 40th Army, that included many Uzbeks and Tajiks, was under-strength, under-trained and ill-equipped. Recruitment became a problem with some Afghans fighting on the side of the Government, changing sides and joining the rebels. Press-ganging by the Soviet/Afghan Government side became common-place with gangs travelling around rural communities twice a year, once after the sowing season and again following the harvest.

From roughly 25,000 in 1980, by 1982 the number of troops in the 40th Army had risen to around 40,000, and as many as 150,000 by the time of the Soviet withdrawal in 1989. However, throughout the period of the war, it was observed that the Soviet/Afghan Government forces never seemed to fight with the same determination and ferocity as their Afghan brothers on the rebel side.

It soon became clear that this was not a war in the conventional sense, but rather a war between regular troops and insurgents using guerrilla tactics. The mujahideen was illusive, extremely mobile, lightly equipped and familiar with the dangerous terrain. Above all, the rebels were highly motivated and fuelled by a commitment to defend their country, their culture and Islam. In other words, they were performing their religious duty in the form of *Jihad.*

Both sides relied heavily on the gathering of intelligence, but it soon became clear that the 40th Army was hampered by a lack of personnel with adequate language skills. Both sides used the services of secret agents and it was not unusual for the same agent to act as a double, or even triple agent.

While the Soviet and Afghan government forces managed to control the major cities and highroads, the mujahideen were able to hold on to the vast rural areas that made up to 80% of the country. The war was never popular with the people of the USSR and when Mikhail Gorbachev assumed the office of General Secretary of the Communist Party of the USSR in 1985, he made the withdrawal of Soviet troops from Afghanistan a priority. In the October of 1985, he met with the Afghan leader Babrak Karmal, urging him to agree to a power-sharing role with the rebels. At the same time, he announced that there should be a gradual withdrawal of Soviet troops.

It took almost four years before the last Soviet soldier of the 40th Army left Afghan soil, marking the end of the Soviet-War on the 15th February 1989. It is estimated that somewhere between a half and two million Afghan civilians had lost their lives. Around five million refugees fled to Pakistan, Iran and other European countries, with another two million internally displaced. It has also been speculated that the ten-year war, resulting in the loss of many Soviet lives, contributed to the fall of the USSR in 1991.

Civil War: 1992-1996

When President Babrak Karmal failed to unite the country, Gorbachev supported Muhammad Najibullah as his replacement. A member of the Parcham faction, Najibullah had previously been head of KHAD (Afghan Secret Police). He became President in September 1987 and continued to receive Soviet support even after the withdrawal of the 40th Army. His attempts to unite the country, by distancing his government from Communism in favour of Afghan nationalism, came to nothing. When the USSR was dissolved in 1991, aid from Russia ended and Najibullah resigned the following year. He tried to reach India, but failed and was forced to remain in Kabul where he found refuge in the UN headquarters compound until 1996, when he was brutally tortured to death by the Taliban.

When Najibullah resigned in 1992, there had been an attempt to form a coalition of the main mujahideen groups, which at the time numbered around six. However, Gulbuddin Hekmatyar, leader of the Hezb-e Islami faction, refused to join the coalition.

Hekmatyar had been the main beneficiary of US aid on the grounds that he had been a strong anti-Soviet commander during the Soviet-Afghan war. He had also been supported by M16 and Margaret Thatcher. But he had the reputation of being perhaps the most brutal of the Afghan warlords and was often referred to as 'the butcher of Kabul'.

Rather than join with the other mujahideen leaders in a coalition, on the 24th April Hekmatyar headed for Kabul and persuaded the government officials to allow him into the city. Fearing that this might result in Hekmatyar seizing control of the whole city, the joint forces of warlords Ahmad Shah Massoud and Abdul Rashid Dostum ousted him. For several days rival groups fought for control of the city. This was to be the beginning of several years' infighting between the forces of different warlords during which time alliances were formed and just as quickly broken.

Between 1992 and 1994, the government of Burhanuddin Rabbani controlled little more than Kabul and its environs, while the warlords held sway over the rest of the country. The Uzbek warlord General Dostum controlled the North, while the Iranian-backed Shi'a Hazaris ruled the province of Bamiyan. The central and southern parts of the country were controlled by numerous smaller groups.

Throughout the in-fighting, the civilian population suffered most at the hands of the warlords who sold off factories and machinery to Pakistani traders in order to finance their internecine warfare. They seized homes and farms from the people and stole merchandise from the bazaars. And they kidnapped and abused young boys and girls. It is estimated that around 25,000 civilians in Kabul alone, died during the first half of 1994.

The Taliban

The unstable situation in Afghanistan, that started with the fall of King Mohammed Zahir Shah in 1973 and continued throughout the Soviet occupation and the civil war that followed, had led to an exodus of hundreds of thousands of refugees to Pakistan. Many of the refugees were orphans who were placed in Saudi-funded madrassas where they both lived and received an education.

During the same period, Pakistan's 'Inter-Services Intelligence' (ISI) trained some 90,000 Afghans. Many were members of the mujahideen who had been supported by the United States and Saudi Arabia, some of whom later became leaders of the Taliban. The word Taliban means 'students' (plural of talib, meaning student), reflecting the fact that the 'foot-soldiers' of the Taliban were originally students of the Pakistani madrassas.

Mullah Mohammad Omar, who became leader of the Afghan Taliban, is typical of many. Little is known about his life, other than that he came from a poor rural background in the Kandahar

Province and fought with the mujahideen against the Russians. After the withdrawal of the Soviets he returned to his previous occupation of teaching in a madrassa, first in Pakistan and then in Kandahar.

Along with many, he was shocked by the corruption and atrocities committed by the warlords after the fall of Najibullah. It is said that in the spring of 1994 he and a small band of 30 men, rescued two girls who had been captured by the warlords. On another occasion, he rescued a young boy from rape. After this, people increasingly asked him for help, which marks the beginning of the rise of the Taliban.

Within months, some 15,000 students had arrived from Pakistan to join Mullah Omar and by the end of the year the Taliban controlled not only Kandahar but also 12 out of 34 provinces of Afghanistan. In September 1996, the Taliban founded the Islamic Emirate of Afghanistan with Kandahar as its capital and Mullah Omar as Head of State.

From the beginning, Mullah Omar was seen as the champion of the people, as someone who stood up to the warlords. He, and those who joined him, believed that they were purging society from corruption and brutality. The stated aims of the Taliban were to 'restore peace, disarm the population, enforce *Sharia* Law and defend the integrity and Islamic character of Afghanistan' (Ahmad Rashid, *Taliban*). Combined with a strict adherence to the *Sharia* Law, the Taliban also follow *Pashtunwali*, the traditional tribal code of the Pashtun people.

In the early years, the Taliban had been welcomed by many Afghans as liberators who freed them from the tyranny of the warlords. Thousands of young men from the refugee camps and madrassas of Pakistan, as well as *jihadists* from around the Muslim world joined Mullah Omar. In time, however, the people began to resent the brutal, almost medieval regime of Taliban rule.

Taliban Post 9/11

Between 1996 and the attack on the Twin Towers on the 11th September 2001, the Taliban consolidated their power with continued support from Pakistan and Saudi Arabia. The attack of 9/11 was attributed to Osama Bin Laden who was thought at that time to be hiding in Afghanistan under the protection of the Taliban and with the full knowledge of Pakistan.

On the 15th September, President George W Bush gave Pakistani President Pervez Musharraf an ultimatum demanding the handing over of Bin Laden with the words 'you are either with us or against us'. At this point Pakistan officially switched sides in support of the US and her allies in opposition to the Taliban. However, neither Pakistan nor the Taliban were prepared to hand over Osama Bin Laden.

On the 7th October the US began bombing Taliban bases. By the 5th December, Mullah Omar was forced to surrender Kandahar and he escaped into the desert on a motorbike. The Taliban lost between 8,000 and 12,000 fighters but many, including its leaders, managed to escape into the Tora Bora Mountains or across the border into Pakistan's tribal areas where they reformed.

Within weeks of defeating the Taliban the US turned its attention to Iraq. Afghanistan was left a country destroyed by decades of war, with a wrecked economy, a broken infrastructure and the loss of a traditional tribal system that had sustained Afghan society for centuries. Crucially however, thousands of Taliban, including the leaders, had managed to escape.

Conclusion

By the beginning of the 20th Century, there were sporadic uprisings across Russian Central Asia protesting against Imperial rule in general and certain policies in particular. The resettlement of emancipated serfs on Central Asian land, as well as the forced conscription of Central Asian men during World War I, both led to rebellion. The brutal response by Tsar Nicholas II, resulting in the death of almost 200,000 Kazakhs and Kyrgyz, has been described as genocide, an accusation denied by Russia.

The situation changed following the Russian Revolution in 1917. The region now became incorporated into the Union of Soviet Socialist Republics (USSR) and was divided into different Administrative Divisions under Communist rule. Consequently, although small communist parties had existed in Central Asia prior to this time, socialism was strengthened and Communist parties in all Central Asian Soviet Republics assumed far greater power.

Between 1936 and 1939, many Chechen and Crimean Tatars were exiled to Central Asia under Stalin's Great Purge, a move that added to social tensions. During the same period, hundreds of Muslims, escaping Soviet religious persecution, fled to Saudi Arabia. To this day, ethnic Uzbeks and Tajiks living in Saudi Arabia support Muslim communities in Uzbekistan and Tajikistan.

The various modernisation programmes that were introduced by the Soviets came at a cost. Vast agricultural and industrialisation projects damaged the environment, particularly in the region of the Aral Sea. Furthermore, efforts at social reform, especially relating to education and women's rights, were fiercely resisted by conservative Muslims, particularly those of Afghanistan.

It was opposition to reform that became the catalyst for the outbreak of the Soviet-Afghan War of 1979-89. With Soviet support, the Afghan government and the PDPA (People's Democratic Party of Afghanistan) attempted to introduce legislation that conflicted with the traditional conservative Islamic values of the majority rural population of the country.

Various opposition groups, collectively known as the mujahideen, formed around different warlords. At the same time, the PDPA was split into two separate factions. As the situation worsened, the Afghan Government appealed to the USSR for military aid to fight the mujahideen. Initially, the Soviets would only commit to the supply of munitions and the service of military advisers. But on the 24th December, 1979, Soviet troops marched into Afghanistan.

Although the US and Britain were aware of Soviet movements on the Afghan border, the motive for the invasion was unclear. It has subsequently been concluded that Moscow was probably reacting to the situation on the ground, rather than pursuing an ambitious imperial dream. Whatever the motive, the invasion was opposed by 104 member-states of the United Nations.

The ten-year long war occurred at the height of the Cold War, when relations between the USSR and the West were at an extremely low ebb. Consequently, the war in Afghanistan became something of a proxy war. The United States, Britain, China, Pakistan and Saudi Arabia supported the Sunni Mujahideen and Iran supported the Shi'a Mujahideen. On the opposing side, the forces of the USSR and the Democratic Republic of Afghanistan were supported by East Germany.

The war proved to be inconclusive and when the Soviet troops finally withdrew in 1989, the country returned to a state of Civil War. The various warlords, who had previously fought against the Soviets, immediately filled the power vacuum. The warlords now fought each other, terrorising the people in the process.

It was in this context that the Taliban, many of whom had been young Afghan refugees from Saudi-backed Pakistani madrassas, came to the aid of the people. They were initially welcomed as liberators and by 1996, having secured large swathes of the country, the Taliban proclaimed the Emirate of Afghanistan which was to be governed by strict Shar'ia law.

On September 11th, 2001, when the Twin Towers were blown up by Islamic terrorists, Osama Bin Laden was suspected as being the mastermind behind the attack. He was thought to be hiding in Afghanistan under the protection of the Taliban. The US began bombing Taliban bases in the October and by December 2001 the majority of the Taliban, including their leaders, had escaped.

11th September, 2001, more commonly referred to as 9/11, proved to be a watershed in world history. In many ways the date marked a change in the relationship between Islam and the rest of the world. This is especially true for Central Asia where the majority of the people are Muslim. For centuries, the region has been subject to invasion, occupation and colonialism. Today, young nation-states are deciding their own futures and finding their own place in a region that still retains the romance of the ancient Silk Road.

*****

EPILOGUE

For most of its history, Central Asia has been ruled by powerful dynasties, fallen under the vassalage of neighbouring empires or been invaded by foreign powers. Only the more remote, inaccessible tribal areas have maintained a degree of independence. However, since the fall of the Soviet Union in 1991, five distinct independent nation states have emerged that are now generally referred to as 'Central Asia', namely Uzbekistan, Tajikistan, Turkmenistan, Kazakhstan and Kyrgyzstan.

Regardless of who has been in power over the centuries, the one constant has been the significance of the land bridge that straddles the region connecting Europe and Asia, otherwise known as the Silk Road, or Roads. In ancient times, silks and spices travelled westwards, while furs, wools and precious metals took an eastward route. Consequently, those who controlled the trade-route accrued immense wealth.

This land bridge, or Silk Road, is now being revitalised. But rather than silks and spices, today the commodities being transported include natural gas, oil, minerals and communication systems and just as in ancient times, China remains the prime mover.

During a visit to Central Asia in September 2013, the Chinese President Xi Jinping raised the initiative of jointly building the Silk Road Economic Belt and the 21st-Century Maritime Silk Road, which was to be known as the Belt and Road initiative. According to the official Chinese Government's website, (*The State Council, The People's Republic of China*, March 30 2015):

> *"Accelerating the building of the Belt and Road can help promote the economic prosperity of the countries along the Belt and Road and regional economic cooperation, strengthen exchanges and mutual learning between different civilizations, and promote world peace and development."*

Although presented as a joint initiative, the reality is that such a project would be in the best interests of China. According to an article in the *Diplomat,* dated 1st February, 2020 ('Potholes and Bumps Along the Silk Road Economic Belt in Central Asia' by Li-Chen Sim and Farkhod Aminjonov), currently 80% of China's imports, including over 50% of its oil from the Middle East, arrive by sea.

Although the Maritime Silk Road, which focusses upon the ASEAN (Association of Southeast Asian Nations), should improve the Republic's maritime trade, it will still not match America's maritime superiority. Consequently, China needs a more secure route for her energy supplies and is therefore putting greater emphasis on the Silk Road Economic Belt (SREB), which would provide an overland link between China, Central Asia, Russia and Europe (the Baltic).

Central Asia plays a key role in this initiative, not just because it provides a 'bridge', as in previous centuries, but because the region is valuable in and of itself. It has rich hydrocarbon and mineral resources, as well as rare earth and metals that are used, among other things, for solar panels and rechargeable batteries, all of which are vital to China's economic growth.

China offers Central Asian countries generous loans in order to develop local infrastructure, such as roads and railways. In most cases, these loans take no account of political, economic or human rights issues. Consequently, they are attractive to authoritarian regimes and Sim and Aminjonov claim that few go through a tender process and up to 30% of funding is lost through corruption.

It is further observed that the local population does not necessarily benefit from Chinese-funded projects. For example, over 80% of workers on a Central Asian project may be migrant Chinese, while less than 10% of the jobs go to the local population. On the other hand, under a multi-national project, less than 30% of jobs would go to the Chinese, with over 40% to local people. The conclusion is that while multi-national, or Western projects, are more transparent, they remain at a disadvantage because they are not able to match the level of funding offered by China.

Chinese influence in Central Asia is typified by the fact that the Republic controls over a quarter of oil production in Kazakhstan and most of Central Asian's natural gas is imported to China through the CA-China gas pipeline that was constructed with Chinese loans. Another example would be SREB funding for Uzbekistan's first nuclear power plant, which is also receiving financial support from Russia. Perhaps a more worrying sign is that China appears to be moving from a 'soft-power' approach, through economic assistance, to 'hard-power' projects such as airports and military bases.

According to the American Enterprise Institute's China Global Investment Tracker, China has invested almost $26 billion in the region since the launch of the BRI in 2013. Other estimates put the figure much higher, with a possible $60 billion in trade deals over the same period.

As the level of Central Asian debt has increased, with a corresponding amount of Chinese involvement in the five Central Asian countries, anti-Chinese protests are growing across the region. Apart from concern over the level of debt, people are calling for a reduction in Chinese work permits. A situation is emerging whereby the people of Central Asia could be open to alternative economic partners, particularly from the West.

From the outset, China had hoped that the positive image of the Belt and Road Initiative, together with generous loan packages, would divert attention away from the Republic's poor reputation concerning the Muslim population of Xinjiang Province. While the plight of the Uyghurs in Xinjiang has received world-wide condemnation, it is of particular concern to fellow Muslims of Central Asia. Alongside the Xinjiang issue, the rights of the people of Hong Kong and deteriorating trade relations with the USA, China's reputation world-wide has recently suffered a further blow due to the Coronavirus, with accusations that the

Republic withheld vital information during the early stages of the outbreak in Wuhan Province.

China's status in Central Asia is being closely watched by both Russia and the USA. The Russians are especially concerned over China's subtle shift from a 'soft power' approach to 'hard power' projects, typified by China's opening, in April 2020, of an airport in the Xinjiang-Uyghur Autonomous District that is dangerously close to the borders with Afghanistan and Tajikistan. China claims that this is the first of many airports to be built in the region that are intended to promote tourism. Russia, on the other hand, sees this as an opportunity for China to access the people and resources of a much-contested region.

As China's involvement in Central Asia has become more aggressive, Russia's response has been to reassess her relationship with her erstwhile ally. Consequently, Moscow is making efforts to counter-balance Chinese activities. For example, in recent years, Russia has justified her military presence at the Kant Air Base, in Kyrgystan, as being necessary to combat Islamist terrorism. However, judging by the equipment at the Base, Russia's presence appears to be more about territorial security backed by military might, than combatting terrorism.

Similar moves have taken place in Tajikistan. According to Paul Goble's article 'Russian Military Seeking to Counter Growing Chinese Role in Central Asia' (June 18, 2020, *Jamestown Foundation*), Tajikistani security expert Muslim Buriyev, says that, "until recently, there existed a balance between Russia and China in the region. Moscow was "responsible" for security, while Beijing spearheaded regional investment. Now, however, the Chinese have shown that Central Asia has ceased to be only a zone of economic interests for them, and they are gradually building up their military cooperation there.".

Until recently, America's interest in Central Asia was generally seen through the prism of either Russia's involvement in the region, or Afghanistan and the War on Terror. In 2011, for example, Hilary Clinton, then Secretary of State, proposed a New

Silk Road initiative. Known as the Lapis Lazuli project, the aim was to create a sustainable Afghanistan, after the withdrawal of US troops, through regional trade, transit and infrastructure projects. Crucially, it would provide a trade and transport route from Afghanistan, via Turkmenistan, Azerbaijan and Georgia, to Turkey.

In recent years, as China continues to make inroads into the region, America has come to realise that the Central Asian states are geopolitically significant in their own right. Consequently, in February 2020, Washington released its own Central Asian strategy.

According to its Policy Objectives:

> *"the United States will work with Central Asian states to build their resilience to short and long-term threats to their stability; to strengthen their independence from malign actors; and to develop political, economic, and security partnerships with the United States. U.S. development efforts should foster regional independence and not create dependency.*

Specific objectives include: joint military training to reduce terrorist threats; to support stability in Afghanistan and to promote United States investment in and development of Central Asia. In order to achieve these aims, over $34 million dollars was to be put aside for economic connectivity and the environment, as well as $90 million for border security. Since 1991, over 40,000 Central Asian students have received American funding and over a million Central Asians visit the United States each year, thereby indirectly strengthening American influence in the region.

American strategy, and that of Russia, is often couched in terms of countering terrorism. But Islamic radicalism in Central Asia is far less a threat than in other parts of the world. This is partly because Islam was suppressed during the Soviet period and is now non-sectarian. Furthermore, although some Central Asians were known to have joined ISIS in Syria and Iraq, their number amounted to no more than about 1,000. (Radio Free

Europe/Radio Liberty, *State, Religion and Radicalism in Central Asia,* November 2014)

Putting aside the threat of terrorism, America's Central Asian strategy appears to have two main aims. First, to counter-balance that of China in terms of trade and second, to secure a stable Afghanistan. Since Western forces have gradually been withdrawing from Afghanistan, America is now encouraging the five Central Asian States to work closely with the country. The fear is that a weak Afghanistan would be vulnerable to advances from Russia, China or perhaps even a rising nationalist India. Each of these countries, as well as Islamic terrorism, could be described as *'malign actors'*, as referred to in the United States Strategy for Central Asia 2015-2019 policy document.

Today, the countries of Central Asia are in a stronger position than in recent history. No longer are they simply gatekeepers of a trade route, whose loyalty and co-operation has been sought by more powerful neighbours. Today, Central Asia consists of independent nation-states that are rich in natural resources. Moreover, these resources are in great demand by the developed world. Consequently, the people of Central Asia are in a position to be able to choose their own trade and political partners.

While China appears to have the greatest financial influence in the region, the United States is now putting considerable effort into count-balancing China's power. Russia still maintains a degree of cultural influence in the region, but is no match for China or the United States.

Perhaps the people of Central Asia will do what they always have done. They will ally themselves with whoever offers the best deal at any one time, while still remaining fiercely independent. The big question is, 'will they look to the East or the West; to China or the United States?'. If they remain true to their history, they will probably keep their options open, and manage both.

*****

WHO'S WHO

Abu Bakr	First Caliph of the Rashidun
Abdul Rashid Dostum	Vice President of Afghanistan 2014-Feb 2020
Ada	Queen of Halicarnassus
Ahmad Shah Durrani	Founder of Afghanistan, 1747
Alexander Burnes	Scottish Explorer and Diplomat
Alexius I Comnenus	Byzantine Emperor, 1081-1118
Ali ibn Abi Talib	Fourth Caliph of the Rashidun, son-in-law of Muhammad
Alp Arslan	Sultan of the Great Seljuk Empire, 1063-1072
Andragorus	Satrap of Parthia
Antiper	Diadochi, General of Greece
Apama	Daughter of Spitamenes and wife of Seleucus I
Ardashir	Founder of Sassanid Dynasty
Arrian	Greek historian Flavius Arrianus Xenophon
Arrhidaeus	Half-brother of Alexander the Great
Astyages	King of Median Empire
Babrak Kamal	Gen Sec, People's Dem Republic of Afghanistan, 1979-1986
Baibars	Sultan of Mamluk Dynasty, 1260-1277
Barsine	Widow of Memnon, satrap of Rhodes
Bucephalus	Alexander the Great's horse
Cassander	Member of Diadochi

Craterus royal family	Member of Diadochi, Guardian of
Croesu	King of Lydia
Cyrus II, the Great BCE	Founder of Achaemenid Empire, 550
Darius I, the Great 486 BCE	King of Achaemenid Empire, 522-
Diodotus	Satrap of Bactria
Dost Mohammad Khan 63	Emir of Afghanistan, 1823-39, 1845-
Genghis Khan 1206-1368	Founder of the Mongol Empire
Ghassanids	Tribal state in Arabia
Gulbuddin Hekmatyar Hezb-e Islami	Afghan politician and leader of
Hasan	Grandson of Muhammad
Hassan-i-Sabbah Assassins	Founder of the Order of the
Hoelun	Mother of Genghis Khan
Husain	Grandson of Muhammad
Herodotus	Greek Historian, 484-425 BCE
Hulagu	Son of Tolui, Khan of the Ilkhanids
Jebe	General in Mongol army
Jochi	Son of Genghis Khan
Khalid ibn Walid	General in Rashidun army
Khosrau I	Shah of Sassanid Empire, 531-579
Khosrau II	Shah of Sassanid Empire 590-628
Kilij Arslan	Seljuk Sultan of Rum, 1092-1107

Kublai Khan Dynasty, 1260-1294	Great Khan and Emperor of Yuan
Lakhmids	Tribal state in Arabia
Malik Shah I 1092	Sultan of the Seljuk Empire, 1072-
Menander I Soter	Indo-Greek King
Memnon	Greek satrap of Rhodes
Mithridates I	King of Parthia, 171-132 BCE
Mithridates II	King of Parthia 124-88 BCE
Mohammed Daoud Khan	President of Afghanistan 1973-1978
Mongke Khan 1259	Great Khan of Mongol Empire, 1251-
Mountstuart Elphinstone	Scottish Statesman and Historian
Muawiyah	First Caliph of the Umayyads
Muhammad Najibullah	President of Afghanistan 1987-1992
Muhammad Taraki	President of Afghanistan 1978-1979
Mullah Mohammad Omar 1996-2001	Mujahideen Commander of Taliban
Nader Shah	Shah of Persia, 1736-1747
Nizam al-Mulk 1092	Vizier of the Seljuk Empire, 1064-
Ogedei	Son of Genghis Khan
Olympias of Alexander the Great	Wife of Philip of Macedonia, mother
Parysatis	Persian wife of Alexander the Great
Perdiccas Arrhidaeus	Member of Diadochi, Regent to
Philip II	King of Macedonia, 359-336 BCE

Porus	King of Indian region of the Hydaspes River in the Punjab
Qutuz	Sultan of Mamluk Dynasty 1259-1260
Ranjit Singh	Ruler of the Sikh Empire 1801-1839
Romnos IV Diogenes 1068-1071	Emperor of the Byzantine Empire,
Saladin	(An-Nasir Salah ad-Din Yusuf ibn Ayyub), Sultan of Ayyubid Dynasty
Sa'd ibn Abi Waqqa	General in Rashidun Army
Seleucus I	Founder of Seleucid Empire, 312-63 BCE
Shah Ismail I	Founder of Safavid Empire, 1501-1736
Shah Tahmasp I	Shah of Persia, 1524-1576
Shah Shujah Durrani	Fifth Emir of Afghan Durrani Empire, King of Afghanistan
Shapur	Shah of Sassanid Empire
Shaybani Khan	Founder of Shaybani Dynasty, Ruler of Khanate of Bukhara
Sisygambis	Mother of Darius III
Sorghaghtani Beki	Wife of Tolui, son of Genghis Khan
Spitamenes	Sogdian warlord
Stateira I	Wife of Darius III
Stateira II	Daughter of Darius III and wife of Alexander the Great
Stratonice	Wife of Seleucus
Temujin	Birth name of Genghis Khan

Timur	(Tamurlane) founder of the Timurid Dynasty 1370-1507
Tokhtamysh	Leader of the Blue Horde
Tolui	Fourth son of Genghis Khan
Umar ibn al-Khattab	Second Caliph of the Rashidun
Uthman ibn Affan	Third Caliph of the Rashidun
William Moorcroft	English explorer employed by the East India Company
Xenophon	Greek Historian, 431-354 BCE
Yasa	Mongol Law
Yazdegerd II	Shah of Sassanid Empire 435-457
Yazdegerd III	Shah of Sassanid Empire 632-651
Yesugei	Father of Ghengis Khan
Yeuzhi	Nomadic tribes from Northern China

*****

WORKS REFERRED TO

A History of Islam in Central Asia, Javad Haghnavaz, pub American International Journal of Research in Humanities, Arts and Social Sciences,

Abbott, Jacob, *Cyrus the Great Makers of History,* pub Harper & Brothers, 1904

Abbott, Jacob, *Darius the Great Makers of History,* pub Harper & Brothers, 1904

Arrian, *The Campaigns of Alexander* (Classics Book 253)

Azizov, Ulugbek *Freeing from the "Territorial Trap", Re-reading the Five Stans Central Asian Spatial Discourse,* Munster, 2015

Biran, Michal *Chinggis Khan,* One World Publications, London 2013

Braithwaite, Rodric, *Afgantsy: The Russians in Afghanistan,* 1979-89, Profile Books, 2011

Burnaby, Frederick: *A Ride to Khiva: Travels and adventures in Central Asia*, Enhanced Media 2017

Burnes, Alexander, *Travels to Bokhara: a Voyage up the Indus to Lahore and a Journey to Cabool, Tartary & Persia,* Vol 1, Enhanced Media 216

Dalrymple, William, *Return of a King: The Battle for Afghanistan*, pub Bloomsbury

Encyclopaedia Iranica

Freeman, Philip, *Alexander the Great,* pub Simon & Schuster

Grainger, John, *The Rise of the Seleukid Empire, 323-223 BC,* pub Pen & Sword History 2014

Hopkirk, Peter, *The Great Game, On Secret Service in High Asia,* pub John Murray 1990

Hopkirk, Peter, *Foreign Devils on the Silk Road: The Search for the Lost Treasures of Central Asia,* pub John Murray 1980

International Journal of Central Asian Studies Vol. 3 1998

Iran Chamber Society

Lewis, Bernard, *The Assassins*, Phoenix, 2003

Maalouf, Amin, *Samarkand*, Hachette Digital, 1989

Martin Ewans, Ed. *The Great Game: Documents,* Routledge, 2004

Mann, John, *Genghis Khan: Life, Death and Resurrection,* pub Bantum 2005

Marozzi, Justin, *Tamerlane, Sword of Islam, Conqueror of the World,* Harpers 2005

Sale, Florentia, *Lady Sale's Afghanistan,* pub Leonaur 2009

Xenophon, *Cyropaedia, The Education of Cyrus,* Translated by F M Stawell

*****

ABOUT THE AUTHOR

Anne has had a life-long interest in history and the religions of the world. This led to her studying both topics for her first Degree and later for her Doctorate. She spent several years living overseas and this experience added to her fascination with people of different Faiths and cultures.

For many years Anne was Adviser in Inter Religious Relations with the Church of England. She was also Vice Moderator of the Dialogue Unit of the World Council of Churches in Geneva and has sat on numerous advisory bodies for Inter Religious Relations around the world. In recognition of her work in this field she was made an Honorary Canon of Chelmsford Cathedral.

Anne lectures regularly on cruise ships as well as many organisations around the United Kingdom.

As well as travelling, she now enjoys writing short, accessible books, many of which have been based on her lectures. This book is the tenth in the *'In Brief' Series: Books for Busy People.*

*****

Printed in Great Britain
by Amazon

76771525R00118